T0123385

THE ROAD LESS TRAVELED

A MEMOIR OF ADOPTION, SPECIAL NEEDS, DETOURS, AND LOVE

Heidi Renee

WESTBOW
PRESS®
A DIVISION OF THOMAS NELSON
& ZONDERVAN

Author photo by Steph Johnson-Beloit, Wisconsin
Family photo by Harmony Images-Amy Sprengel New Berlin, Wisconsin
Cover photo by Heidi Renee

WestBow Press books may be ordered through booksellers or by contacting:

WestBow Press
A Division of Thomas Nelson & Zondervan
1663 Liberty Drive
Bloomington, IN 47403
www.westbowpress.com
1 (866) 928-1240

ISBN: 978-1-5127-4561-0 (sc)
ISBN: 978-1-5127-4562-7 (hc)
ISBN: 978-1-5127-4560-3 (e)

Library of Congress Control Number: 2016909809

Print information available on the last page.

WestBow Press rev. date: 7/7/2016

Contents

Dedication

To my sweet baby boy. May you always know the love
I have for you as your Mommy,
and as your advocate.

Two roads diverged into a wood and I-I
took the one less traveled by,
and that has made all the difference.
~Robert Frost

Introduction

The basic makeup for a road trip is simple. People + Vehicle + Destination = Epic Travels. The people and vehicles will vary, as will the destinations. Some will choose the highway, while others will choose the scenic route. Some will drive fast, others will take the Sunday drive approach. Neither is right. Neither is wrong. Most likely, both will be full of imperfections, GPS recalculations, detours, and surprises. All will most certainly be memorable.

We dive into these explorations of the open road either prepared or nonchalant. I have learned, and am still learning to enjoy the road with our son. I've become comfortable with throwing the map out the window—when deemed necessary. Muddy and refreshing, my journey has opened my eyes wider than I ever imagined.

Our story is not the perfect "couple adopts child and lives happily ever after" story. It is full of many imperfections, detours, flat tires, joy, wonder, and most of all, love. Where the unexpected was met with immense heartache and tenderness. Ever changing. Ever blessed. The Road Less Traveled.

~This book is a compilation of my private thoughts combined with excerpts from my current blog.

CHAPTER 1

Dead End

Confession: I really thought we had this baby thing in the bag.

First comes love, then comes marriage, then comes the baby....

Our story began as many do. Boy meets girl. Boy and girl talk. Boy and girl fall in love. Boy and girl get married. Boy and girl try to have a family. Boy and girl fail. Oops.

We took quite the detour from what we had learned and interpreted to be the traditional path of life. The world of baby-making has what I call white-picket fence syndrome. I fell for it. You find that perfect guy or girl, buy the perfect house, with the white picket fence, and have the perfect kids. Those perfect kids should come easy. *No sweat.* It should just happen, shouldn't it? It is the next, natural step in building your family. It is supposed to just happen.

Naturally.

Dare I say the word....easy?

Isn't it?

No one warned me how the beautiful experience of getting pregnant is rudely squashed by the world of infertility. Everything about this new world was cold and robotic. We were abruptly inviting multiple strangers on this very intimate journey. I didn't want to let go of the intimacy, but I was eager for success. *It's going to be fine.*

The warm October sun poured in through the car window. Sun or no sun, my nerves were anything but cheery. They were tight, and I gripped my coffee with a fierce fear of what was about to happen. The light, all of it, seemed to disappear as we pulled into the parking structure.

The fertility clinic was as I suspected; cold and staunch. Jeremy had gone with his specialist, and me with mine. Tears began to well as I waited my turn. *Why am I crying on this stupid cotton-pickin' table? She hasn't even touched me yet.* I spent the duration of the exam fighting tears and shaking, trying to show the big bad specialist I was tough enough for the job.

Is this a job? A process? This doesn't feel maternal.

She started rattling off the next steps in my "fertility journey" like it was a grocery list. This was my body and certainly my soul, not a list of any kind.

"She's the best", I told Jeremy. As we sat in her office, stacks of unorganized files surrounded us. *We're a number.* I found myself completely distracted by those files and her cold flat announcements.

"We will do intrauterine insemination (IUI), which usually runs up to three rounds, then in vitro fertilization (IVF), then…" *Then, then, then….* I didn't expect hand-holding. It's a procedure. It's medical. Whatever. But as the list rattled on, we both felt uneasy and stared at each other with quiet yearning of wanting to hit the panic button and run for the hills. We hadn't even discussed IVF and she made it sound like it was cemented into our plan.

So natural. So next step.

A few weeks later the phone rang. I heard the girl on the line gently say, "Your husband's lab results came back. IUI is a waste of your time. You would have a less than ten percent chance with IVF. Okay? Goodbye."

Someone had screwed my feet into the floorboards. I sobbed uncontrollably as I shuffled to our bedroom. A few seconds later the phone rang again. My heart sunk deep, having a deep and correct hunch of who was calling and why. Friends had called to share their joyous news of expecting their first child.

Now? Why now? They couldn't have called later? Stupid body. Stupid procedures.

Someone had just poured salt directly into the fresh, raw wound that was my heart. I couldn't breathe. I couldn't speak. I wanted to scream and melt into a puddle simultaneously. That beautiful experience was now a nightmare.

IVF was out of the question. We were firm in that decision long beforehand. We could not justify spending an astronomical amount of money on something that was doomed to fail. Spend a huge amount of money for a ten percent chance of success. *I don't think so.*

We stayed stagnant for a few months. We also began to share our fertility struggles publicly. That's when the stories began to pour in. So-and-so got pregnant because her husband sat on a frozen bag of peas before sex. Stand on your head. Do twenty jumping jacks. Boxers not briefs. Drink heavily and it will happen. You name it, we heard it.

I didn't want to hear any of it.

Slowly we began to consider domestic adoption. Jeremy had a friend who had great success with not one but two domestic adoptions. We attended an information meeting that a local adoption agency was offering. My heart was pounding as we walked into that meeting. I wanted all the details. *If I ask too many questions I'm going to look like a crazy woman.* How does this work? What about the birthparents? What is TPR (termination of parent rights)? How much does this all cost? *Give me the details!*

A few weeks later we filled out the paperwork and sent it in. After waiting what seemed like an agonizing three months, we received a call from the agency stating we'd be doing all three of our interviews, individual meetings, and our home study within the next two weeks. *Panic mode.*

All the uncertainty of riding Space Mountain hit me like a ton of bricks. We bought a family vehicle, and new furniture, and had new carpet and flooring installed. The nursery was cleaned out and a space was clearly allocated for baby-to-be. "You are a great fit, a great match. It won't be long before a birthmother will choose you", they said.

Our interviews flew by. Following the list of requirements, I bought a new smoke detector and double-checked the stability of the stair handrail down to the basement. We wanted everything to be perfect for our home study and safe for our new little bundle of joy. *I hope we pass the test.* The morning of our home study our carpet installers were still installing the new carpet. I was frantically moving the new furniture into the rooms they had finished. As the last of the installers were pulling out of the driveway the phone rang. Two hours before our home study, our social worker called to tell us we were no longer a good fit for the program. No explanation. No anything. Nothing.

My legs went numb. I stopped breathing as the tears started to stream down my face. I hung up the phone in disbelief and stood frozen in that hallway. *Again.*

Eventually I called Jeremy at work to tell him and collapsed onto that brand new chaise I had just pushed into the living room. *This is not happening. This is not happening. What did we do wrong?* I sobbed uncontrollably into my favorite quilt. The octagon patterns were fraying and beginning to fall apart. *Just as I was.*

No one had warned me how the adoption process wrecks you. No one had warned me how adoption puts all of your eggs in someone else's basket and then you hand that basket over to decide your parental fate. No one had warned me about the constant self-doubt and constant reflection. The worry and lack of control. Someone else makes the determination if you are a good match. A good fit. Worthy. Qualified. Up to par. Someone else decides whether or not you become a parent.

CHAPTER 2

Caution

I have often imagined how the "traditional" way of making a baby would be skewed by the often ridiculous process of adoption. How ridiculous would it be to have a large packet of paperwork, including a hefty fee, plastered on your bedroom door with a sign reading "do not enter until all paperwork is completed, submitted, reviewed, submitted again, all fees paid, and approval is received."

It seems ridiculous; because it is ridiculous.

I am indeed a rule follower. I haven't always been, but it has become my default. When my heart gets involved, I begin to dissect and evaluate said rules.

Sharing the news we were "out of the program" was horrid.

Well why? What's wrong with them?!

Tell them to go pound sand (my personal favorite expression I heard).

Well they're jerks anyhow.

Thanks, that somehow makes it all better.

"Chalk it up to idiocy and move on folks" was the underlying message I was receiving.

If only it had been that easy.

Who had given a faceless organization the right to determine whether we were going to parents or not?

Who had given them permission to pour scalding hot water on our life plans?

We tried to pick up the pieces and move forward…but not knowing where you are moving to makes one's efforts rather challenging. Staying stationary was predictable and avoided pain.

On the day the cradle was taken out of the nursery I screamed in anger.

Why was this happening?

We sat for a few months, putting all our efforts into breathing and functioning. The very things that are required for daily living were beyond consuming. A mother's broken heart is no joke. During a general phone conversation with Jeremy's cousin Marty, we began to ask questions about adoption. He and his wife Michele had adopted their children internationally a few years earlier. We asked rapid-fire questions to which we received truthful, heartfelt answers. We decided it wouldn't hurt to request information from a few other, bigger, local agencies, this time with our focus on international adoption.

I remembered the car salesman we had bought our bright, shiny new family vehicle from. He had mentioned that he and his wife had adopted and that his wife was a social worker, working for a local adoption agency. I called her. Her name was Dee and she sounded friendly on the phone. Spring found us sitting on the couch in Dee's office. We were both feeling ten times more nervous than we had been the first time.

We had already been rejected once.

To trust or not to trust?

She asked what brought us to her. We shared our journey like a heaping spoonful of casserole on your plate. It was sort of a verbal vomit. We shared what we had encountered with our first adoption agency. She shook her head with disbelief. Her reaction solidified that we had been working with the wrong people. What had transpired was not normal. She talked us through what the current forecast of adoptions by country and gave us information regarding international adoption.

After doing some general research online, we were already leaning toward Guatemala. Guatemalan children were coming home as infants and were well-cared for in private orphanages. The process was simplistic compared to many other countries and the travel requirements were doable for us. She shared that if we chose Guatemala we'd have to use another agency for placement. Meaning, we'd have to use another agency as our connection to Guatemala, using their Guatemalan attorney and following their program requirements. This began the first of many references to the phrases "home study agency" and "placement agency". We poured through the packets of information we left her office with, held our breath, and jumped in.

Jumping in was exciting, terrifying, and healing all at the same time. We began our home study requirements with Deb and also began the application process with our placement agency in another state. While the requirements of our local agency were rather simple, we still worried about our home study. Deb walked us through the process and what would happen on that fateful day. She told us we would be fine!

Sure.

I'll trust you at an arm's length, thank you.

Deb told us the only thing we'd need to make sure of was that there weren't any safety hazards in our house-no faulty railings on any stairways -and make sure to have the smoke detector in the child's room. Suddenly I felt a little ahead of the game.

Deb was right. The interviews were free flowing conversations, full of honesty, true reservations, and open-hearted thoughts. The home study was a breeze. It didn't really matter that I had spent hours cleaning and perfecting our home. Even after she assured us, as she was walking out our front door that we had passed the test, we still held our breath until her report came in the mail.

There is one element of the adoption world that is a well-kept secret that will consume your life. What's the secret? *Paper.* I spent hours and hours and hours filling out paperwork. They wanted to know everything about us. Our family histories, health status, income, and assets. We each wrote autobiographies to become parents. I felt like the only detail missing was how many times we went to the bathroom each day. We filled out questionnaires and answered countless questions.

What age of child would you accept?

What kind of child are you willing to accept?

What is your reason for adopting? I restrained Jeremy from solely answering this question. *Sarcasm plus applying for international adoption equals potential disaster without proper editing.*

His sense of humor was refreshing and necessary in such a sea of rules and requirements. We had background checks, applications for passports, and fingerprinting done by the United States Naturalization and Immigration Service as well as the FBI, along with an application to adopt an international orphan. Each document needed to be notarized, authenticated, and apostilled. I didn't know what authentication or apostilling was until I read those words on our "to be completed" checklist.

If I worked for an adoption agency, I would also share with parents the hidden cost of adoption. Sure, you read the general information sheet on your country of choice and see the program fee, travel fees, and agency fees. But they should include the postage, copying, faxing, gas, and mileage. The "hoops" cost money too (notarizations, apostilling, authenticating, fingerprinting). When our certificates were authenticated and apostilled, they became a work of art. They were so beautiful. I would have taken color copies of them, except I already felt like Big Brother was watching me. I wanted to keep some of them for nostalgia. Once our checklist was complete, all of our documents were put together in a packet and sent to our placement agency. From there, another risk. Mailing our entire lives together to Guatemala.

Dear God, please let this get there in one piece. These are all original documents, with their fancy schmancy signatures, stamps, and impressions. Please, please, please. Thanks, God. Heidi

CHAPTER 3

Green Light

It was a beautiful day in September. I was home, attempting to take a nap when the phone rang. Our phone had a "let me say out loud who is calling" feature, which most of the time was incredibly annoying. That day, it sent my heart beating into overdrive when it rang at 2:38pm. It was our placement agency. I *literally* ran and slid down the hall in my socks, Tom Cruise in *Risky Business* style, and missed the phone call. While trying to call them back, I received a busy signal. I checked my email while listening to my new voicemail. *Heidi, check your email, we have a referral for you. Click.* After a few rounds of cat and mouse via phone calls, mixed with wild tears of joy on my end, we finally connected. She repeated all of the information I had speedily read in her email, which I hastily scribbled down:

A baby boy had been born three months earlier in a small town in Guatemala. He was born early and tiny, weighing between 3 and 4 pounds. He spent some time in the hospital immediately following his birth. He is a happy, healthy little boy. And cute too, might I add.

I was shaking. She assured me pictures were on the way.

Ok. Ok. Ok. Breathe.

A few precious moments later, I became a mom. The intense emotion that filled my veins was as sweet as nectar and packed with adrenaline. I could have run a marathon filled with all of this love for a child I hadn't even met yet. There he was, in all his cuteness. Button nose, in his blue sleeper, curled up in his bouncy seat. He was smiling while sleeping, displaying nothing but sweet, sweet innocence. His seat was placed on colored mats. I memorized the color order of those mats. *Green. Yellow. Red. Blue.* That's what happens when your only connection to your son is through a photograph. As I waited for more pictures to enter my inbox, I stared happily at my baby boy staring at me across the screen. I was officially a mom. This child was born into my heart, the very moment I laid eyes on him. If you had tried to explain this feeling to me beforehand, I really couldn't have understood it. Because the world finds folly and ridiculousness with the notion that you can love a child who lives half way across the world…one that you've never, ever met.

After trying to compose myself, I decided to try and surprise Jeremy. *Surprise, you're a dad! Well, something to that effect.* I called him at work, while simultaneously attaching a picture to an email that should have arrived in his inbox while we were chatting. I was entirely too calm, so he knew something was up. "Open your email and meet your son," I said.

"It helps if you attach the picture to the email, honey," he said. *Oops.* I am certain that my heart was racing far beyond a normal rate by that point.

My second attempt achieved success and Jeremy laid eyes on his son, I wished in that moment, that we could have shared this huge moment together. Nevertheless, I was grateful to technology for at least allowing us to share our new found joy via phone and email. We decided not to tell anyone until we had chosen a name for our new son.

We had thought about names for our baby for months. We had a boy name picked out, but never decided on a girl name. By the time Jeremy arrived home, more photos of our baby boy arrived in my inbox. A few of them broke my heart, as they showed this beautiful young woman handing this baby boy to one of the caregivers at the orphanage. *Who was she?* Another photo of a tiny, tiny baby with an IV still in his hand was the last picture at the bottom of the email. *Too painful*, I thought. I concentrated my thoughts on Mr. Cuteness in his bouncer. Jeremy and I embraced in our driveway in a different way than ever before. It was new, fresh, and scary. I had replayed in my mind so many ways to share a pregnancy with him and then morphed that into sharing a referral with him. The delivery didn't matter, though. We were both ridiculously nervous, yet so excited we could hardly contain ourselves.

We anxiously awaited our baby boy's official referral packet. We were required to review all of his information and then formally accept or reject our referral. *How could we not accept this referral?* We were jolted into parenthood and in that moment-attached at the screen. He was no longer an orphan, he was my son. We cared deeply about his whereabouts, his care, his life, his heart, his every fiber. I cared about the other children he was living with. I wanted to know everything I could within the strict and rigid boundaries of being thousands of miles away.

We named our son Alejandro Jas (j ai s) and decided his nickname would be AJ. He did not resemble a Lucas or Charlie, or any of the other potential names we had pondered. He looked like his birth name.

We began calling family and friends immediately. Our news didn't travel so smoothly at first. People were confused about his name, how to pronounce his name, what his middle name was… *Why don't you rename him? Why don't we give him an American name?* Because he's Guatemalan and he doesn't look like a Steve, Robert, or Joey?!

The next day our packet arrived. Enclosed was a DVD that was shot a few months prior by another adoptive couple with our adoption agency. The DVD showed the hotel we would later stay in, the orphanage, the staff, the attorney, and the adoptive parent's forever moment with their new son. I bawled for hours as I watched this short video over and over and over. Pure love. Pure emotion. Pure awesomeness was shared in what I'm sure was meant to be a more informational DVD rather than emotional. All of this emotion for a DVD that didn't even include footage of my son. That is the power and complexity in loving the orphan.

I felt such a strong connection to this couple; so much so that I wrote them an email of thanks. That email lead to an instant friendship. I needed to thank them for documenting their journey and allowing our agency to share it with other parents waiting on their children. I felt an odd sense of comfort in watching this video. Knowing where AJ was playing, where he was being bathed, what he slept in, what the caregivers looked like, what the orphanage looked like. It was a gift. A gift we watched over and over again.

To keep busy, I brushed-up on my high school Spanish and bought a few books to add to my limited vocabulary. Jeremy was confident that "donde el bano" was all he needed to know. My mom was busy at work making our crib bedding. I had chosen a classic Winnie the Pooh print with sage green, banana yellow, and cloud blue accents during our first adoption attempt. We chose a white crib and changing table. I painted an old dresser white with banana yellow knobs and trim. The nursery was ready even before AJ was a twinkle in our eyes. I was beyond ready to make it HIS.

CHAPTER 4

Merge

Our case entered Guatemalan Family Court after the new year. Our family and friends threw me a fabulous baby shower around the same time. I was humbled by the love poured out on us by so many I was eager to share the ins and outs of adoption with those that attended. I shared new pictures of AJ which had been sent to me the day before. I shared what I had completed of his Lifebook so far and enjoyed the fabulous company. I shared all of the very limited information that I had.

Toward the end of the day, I felt myself becoming irritated with repeating the same lines: *We don't know when he's coming home. I don't know exactly what size he'll be when he comes home. I don't know why his birthmother didn't keep her legs shut (stuffing delicious cake in my mouth to keep me from saying anything else)*. I felt like I was supposed to have all the answers. Clearly I did not. I began to learn that outsider judgments and crude questions awoke the Mama Bear inside me. Not only did I become protective of my son, I became protective over our decision to adopt, our process, as well as my son's birthmother and her choices. This was a response I had not anticipated, in the least. *This is going to be tricky.*

As my car was being packed to the ceiling with our family and friends generosity, I spoke to my baby boy.

You are loved my child, so loved. I hope you feel it.

We received a video solely of AJ in February. The video was only a few minutes, but stirred tears that lasted for hours. It was also our first glimpse of his primary caregiver, Seina. His caregiver just gushed over AJ, which created a soft spot in my heart for her. She showed a true bond with him, and I was thankful. Thankful he was in good hands and being loved. I had heard through the adoption grapevine that preemies were "kangarooed" by orphanage staff. Meaning, they were carried everywhere and smooched on a lot.

A few weeks later we received authorization to travel for our visit trip. *Pack and repack. Pack and repack.* We flew out of O'Hare in the wee hours of the morning, arriving in Guatemala in the mid-afternoon. The temperature, while gorgeous and tropical, was a strict opposite of what we had left in the wintery Midwest.

We arrived at our hotel, which was located in the business zone. The street reminded me of Wisconsin Avenue and Marquette University in downtown Milwaukee. The hotel was a former French mansion, with a handful of rooms and a courtyard dining room full of charm and hospitality. The floors were marble, the rooms adequate, the showers small with exquisite tiling, and everything had that damp "a change in climate" feeling. We were close to the US Embassy, which gave me great comfort, but I also felt uncomfortable as the locals passed by hanging onto the outside of the city buses staring at us. The hotel's atmosphere made for a laid back calm environment; perfect for anxious and emotional prospective adoptive parents. The hotel staff were used to their adoption clientele and provided an amazing amount of support to our nervous souls.

We barely slept. Today was the day we were going to meet our son. I walked up the marble spiral staircase to the front porch of the hotel and wrote a letter to my baby boy:

Today will be one of the happiest days in my life. We are finally going to meet you. Mommy is crying already. We arrived yesterday afternoon and have been in quite a daze. We received a positive DNA match just a few weeks ago and booked our first visit trip as soon as we could. Here we are! We will become three today. Even if that means we have to leave you here for a little while-you still warm my heart like nothing in this world can.

We are staying at a local hotel that is very adoption friendly. There is a beautiful upstairs porch which Mommy is sitting on and writing to you. We will be picked up at 10am to come and see you. Pick you up, and hold you for the first time...

I could have sat on that porch for hours. It was as if time stood still for me and I was sitting watching the world go by. It was so peaceful, yet so loud with the constant buses and traffic passing. The intricate tiles on the floor reminded me of the complex nature of the situation, while the smooth and rounded columns made me smile with the reminder of how love holds us and supports us. After being thousands of miles from him for so long, I was less than ten minutes away from my son. A concept I was trying with all my might to grasp as I sat on that porch.

A few hours later, we were parked in front of the orphanage. We waited for the cold, dark green metal gate to open and pulled in. We entered the orphanage through the rear and were greeted by school age children when we arrived. We were instructed to go upstairs and ask for AJ's caregiver. *Breathe Heidi, just breathe.*

I walked up what seemed to be never-ending stairs and saw a bright, sunlit space filled with bambinos. I hadn't even noticed the rooms off to the right or to the left. My broken Spanish got the point across that we were looking Seina, our son's caregiver.

She came flitting by us, flashing her sweet smile that we had seen before. She motioned for us to follow her into the room on the right. We stood in the doorway, between the light in the hall and the dark room she had walked into. She walked to the row of bassinets on the back wall and picked up a tiny, precious child. We backed into the hallway as she walked towards us.

At first, I thought he was wrong child; he was so small for an eight month old.

And then I saw his sweet, sleepy face.

I knew he was mine.

She handed him to me with gentle care. I wrapped him in my arms and closed my eyes. AJ wrapped his fragile little fingers around my woven purse strap. He snuggled into my chest. I didn't want to move. Neither did my son. My heart was forever sealed to his. I opened my eyes to see my husband beaming with pride. I handed him his son and instantly fell in love with him all over again. There is something about men with their children that stirs this incredible emotion of love inside those of us who love them. Jeremy gently held his son, and smiled in a way I had never witnessed before. Pure joy, nervousness, and love, all combined into one moment. This precious baby boy was all ours for 24 short hours. At the time that was the rule. 24 hours and that's it. His caregiver came floating out of AJ's room speaking Spanish. "Rub the ointment on his legs at night." *Thank heavens for hand gestures.*

We squeezed into the car and drove back to the hotel with another couple and their child. I should probably mention that Guatemala does not require car seats and that their traffic is nothing short of unorganized chaos…fast, unorganized chaos. We began to remove AJ's layers of clothes. Guatemalans dressed much differently than I would have thought for their "Land of Eternal Spring" climate. Often layers and layers of long heavy clothing adorn these kind people. AJ had at least three layers on, along with socks, while the temperature was above sweltering. The socks came off, at least for the car ride. Bare feet were a big no-no, so whenever we were in public we needed to, at the very least, have his socks on his feet.

We arrived back at the hotel and made our way upstairs to our room. Equipped with my trusty travel Spanish phrase book I somehow managed to ask for a crib (which was really a pack and play) and a bathtub completely in Spanish. Up to that point I had not been brave enough to utter anything other than "gracias, por favor, and Buenos Dias." We sat and stared at this baby boy who was real.

Now what?

While seeing a picture of your son is wonderful and has a way of connecting you whether you want it to or not, holding him and seeing him in the flesh was food for the soul. His cheeks were edible, his smile contagious. We played with him, we tickled him. We fed him a bottle, and failed at feeding him cereal. He fell asleep in my arms, with his new pacifier safely secure in his tiny little mouth. I found myself sending never-ending thoughts of thanks for the experiences I had in taking care of children. I was prepared me with a coolness that helped me enjoy this experience with AJ, versus fretting over whether he wanted to eat, sleep, or poop.

We wandered upstairs to the front porch to visit with fellow adoptive families. AJ slept through the night, only waking up once for a bottle. While he did sleep, Mom and Dad didn't. We woke up with his every move. Morning came all too soon, and our visit with AJ was cut short of that full 24 hours. We dragged out our breakfast, gave him the longest bath ever given, and spent some alone time with our son. We literally watched him sleep for two hours before it was time to return him. Return him. As if he was a book borrowed from the library. Even now, eight years later, my stomach turns just thinking about this day.

We packed his bag and sat downstairs on what we adoptive parents had named the "couches of doom". It's where you go to wait when you return your child. I felt like I had just passed through one of those turn-styles at a sporting event, except I had gone in and come right back out. While we were waiting, a family offered to take our picture. We had 1,562 pictures of our son from yesterday alone, but we didn't have any family pictures. There we were, etched in time. Our little family in a Guatemalan hotel, with a beautiful hutch, lace draperies, and the eternal spring sunshine as our backdrop. When I reflect on this photo, I see my husband's joy, my pain, and a precious little boy who didn't notice his photo was being taken. It is our first family photo, one that will forever be engrained in my mind.

All too soon we were walking up to those familiar stairs at the orphanage. With every step, I fought the tears. *I can do this, I thought. We'll be back soon. He's in good hands.* When his caregiver saw him, she instantly lit up like a Christmas tree. *And I stood there.* Like I didn't know what I was supposed to do. I was frozen. She graciously stood and waited for me, without holding out her arms for him. *Thank you.*

The millisecond I pulled AJ away from my chest, I lost it. Complete and utter pain hit me like a truck. I don't remember the transfer of AJ from me to her, but the next thing I knew, I was standing in front of her, childless. She spoke to him in Spanish and he smiled. I stood, bawling and hyperventilating. I have no idea how I turned around to face Jeremy. I was embarrassed, yet my emotions were overpowering my manners. *What a crazy psycho American woman. Why is she crying?* I gently assumed that this whole process of adoptions is normal everyday life for the staff at the orphanage. *Well, this was my life too and this was not normal.* I managed to pair a stuttered thank you together with a fake smile. Jeremy guided me down the stairs, while I continued (without success) to stifle my tears and catch my breath. I couldn't see the stairs through my tears, everything was so blurry. Pure grace landed me on the ground floor.

I continued to sob as we drove away, because the only thing that was worse than handing him back to his caregiver was driving away from the place where he was…and I wasn't. Jeremy placed his arm around me, comforting me. He gave me tissues and squeezed my shoulder with support. After a good mile Jeremy and our driver began lightening the mood by cracking jokes and trying to make me laugh. By the time we reached the hotel again, I was numb. Jeremy requested that the crib and bathtub be taken out of our room, and we spent the next few hours zoning out in the internet cafe.

I had run that moment, that very moment when we would have to return AJ through my head over and over again thousands of times. I'm sure this was in a steep effort to prepare myself for that moment. None of it worked. I could not have seen this wave of emotion coming, even if I tried. We knew we had 24 hours. But 24 hours in theory is different than 20 some hours with your child in your arms. I had bonded with my child and had no choice but to leave him. *What kind of mother does that*, I asked myself. One who is willing to sacrifice, and wait.

CHAPTER 5

Accelerate

A few weeks after we arrive home from our first visit, we received updated pictures. AJ was wearing the same outfit he was wearing when we first met him. The little octopus outfit, which matched the blanket which was in his bag. I felt like a bunny with a carrot. *Here's your son, you can't have him.*

Our adoption case continued to move through the necessary Guatemalan judicial systems. We prayed our case would not receive a previo (a kick-out). Our case was in the last court necessary for approval and was not easy to pass through. One previo sent you spiraling down the adoption paperwork stack. Your time in and waiting before your previo would not count toward your new submission. It was every prospective adoptive parent's nightmare. Once your case was in the last court, the estimated wait time for approval was three weeks to three months. Around this time, a political fire storm began between the Guatemalan and US sides of adoptions. It was assumed it would slow the adoption process. The assumption was correct. Each week more confusing information was released. This worried us, but also bonded us to AJ even more. We had no idea how worried we *should* have been. Once our case was approved by the last court, the new birth certificate would be issued, our baby boy would have a Guatemalan passport, the official adoption decree would be signed, and our case would go back to the US Embassy where we'd await a pink slip. In this case, pink slips were good things. Pink slips gave you a time and date for your child's via appointment at the US Embassy.

With the turbulent political climate surrounding Guatemalan adoptions, Jeremy and I decided another visit trip was in order. The process was becoming even more unpredictable and AJ was going to turn one year old all too soon. If I couldn't have him home, I wanted to be there for my child's first birthday. In fact, I'm not sure my husband had much of a say about the idea of a second visit. *My mommy heart needed to be with her baby boy.* We decided Jeremy would stay home and save his vacation time for our pick-up trip; my mom would come along for the ride instead.

When you travel to a place that is classified as a third-world country, such as Guatemala, a sense of "I want to help" hits you. At least it hit us. We had asked what the orphanage needed as far as supplies before we left. We collected over-the-counter medications and other medical supplies from our generous family and friends, enough to fill one solid suitcase of supplies. Mom and I trekked army duffels and a huge suitcase down the recently polished marble floor of the Guatemalan airport.

June in Guatemala embraced the true meaning of Eternal Spring. The rules for adoption visitation had changed for the better. We had AJ for three whole days. I could barely contain myself with excitement. It was no surprise that AJ was in Seina's arms when we arrived at the orphanage. He was sick with that "I live in a group care setting so I get sick all the time" cold. He was sick during our first visit, but this was the worst I had seen him. My usually happy boy was absolutely miserable. He was lethargic and had a constant runny nose. Despite his schedule reflecting otherwise, he was still on a bottle and *still* wasn't taking solids. Out of frustration I reached out to our agency. They told me to keep trying to feed him with a spoon, insisting this aversion to a spoon and solids was normal. I was beginning to suspect this was anything but normal.

We sat outside in the beautiful courtyard and enjoyed the fountain's mist. My mom bounced AJ up and down from her lap while he grinned and giggled. Life, in that moment, was perfect.

He didn't sleep very long anytime he went down, and didn't like to be fed in our room. I was only able to feed him on the dark green couch in the hallway just outside the door to our room. He hated baths and cried more than he smiled. He wasn't sitting up, nor was he crawling. He was only lying on his stomach, lifting his head and feet in a patterned motion (like a fish) and staring at his fingers. I felt uneasy, and so did Mom.

The second night of our visit, I put AJ to bed, ordered room service for dinner, and went to the internet cafe to check my email and update our website. There was an email from our agency, stating that we should celebrate because our case was approved! Holy buckets! I tried to compose myself, although I am sure I was beaming like headlights. We had many conversations with other waiting families at the hotel about how long it was taking to pass through the last court. The overall mood of our hotel was heartbreaking. While I wanted to, I was not about to run across the courtyard like Julie Andrews in the *Sound of Music*. That would have been cruel. Instead, I contained myself into this fast-paced walk, looking only at the floor or walls as I sped off to our room. I opened the door and bamboozled my own mother, shouting "We're approved!" She shrieked and bounced off the bed toward me. We hugged and cried and looked down at this amazing little boy, who was officially part of our family.

I sprinted to the front desk to ask them to do the things that they do to make international phone calls happen and got the world's newest official Daddy on the line. Oh, how I wished we could celebrate this moment together. *Was this becoming a pattern? No.* Instead, I gave him a list of people to call and inform, told him I loved him, and went on to call my Dad. My Dad was in the middle of his second battle with cancer when we left for Guatemala. I am forever grateful to him for sharing my Mom with me at a time when we both needed her. He was thrilled with our news and reminded me to book an extra plane seat for AJ's cheeks. They were rather chubby and were by far Dad's favorite physical feature of AJ. My heart sung with gladness for our news, but was wrecked with sadness. Listening to my Dad's voice seep his pain and knowing my mother was next to me instead of with him was more than I could swallow.

Despite our joy, the next morning was difficult for me. It was the day before AJ's actual first birthday. Due to "the rules", we could not keep AJ until his birthday. I had packed little plates and party hats and a number "1" candle to celebrate this momentous occasion. Given the overall mood of the hotel, the thought of passing around party hats and cake seemed ineffectual. The cake was a moot point since it was quite clear that AJ was still not eating solid foods.

Instead, I settled on sticking the "1" candle in the most delicious pancakes we had ever had. This viewpoint was not only my own;

Jeremy and my Mom had agreed. They were buttery golden yellow, with a consistency that I have yet to encounter again. This was the traditional breakfast at the hotel, served with eggs, bacon, refried black beans, and a fried plantain. I never did understand why the butter packets were from Switzerland, though. I always thought that was odd.

Mom and I quietly sang "Happy Birthday" to AJ while he fussed and fussed in my arms. It did not make for a happy occasion, which left me heartbroken. This moment was the reason I had come to Guatemala in the first place. Ok, maybe second. I wanted to see my son first; I wanted to celebrate his birthday second.

This was not the way it was supposed to be.

The afternoon rolled around and we were once again meeting our driver out in the front courtyard. Since our adoption case was approved, AJ was our son in the eyes of the Guatemalan government. However, we were not permitted to leave the country with him just yet. We had heard of families flying down and taking custody of their children in-country until they received "pink". Our driver asked if we were going to just stay in country with AJ.

I wish buddy.

Oh how I wished I had just won the lottery and could stay down here until we received that pink slip. I assured him that unfortunately we would be leaving and returning for our US Embassy appointment.

We returned to the orphanage with AJ, where Seina was ecstatic to see him once again. She said a whole lot of fast words in Spanish to both AJ and me, and I just smiled. I'm sure they all thought I was a crazy American woman this time as I wasn't crying as we left. I knew in my heart, that we'd be back to pick AJ up soon.

We were able to spend quite a bit more time at the orphanage than we had our previous visit. We were granted permission to take pictures of several of AJ's friends for other waiting families that Jeremy and I had become close with. Eventually, the monthly pictures and updates became much more sporadic, if at all. We were happy to oblige these parents, as they did the same for us. As parents, we were allowed to send a plastic gallon size storage bag full of items for our child, with their name clearly marked on the front of the bag. We had sent a bag to AJ with another family earlier in our adoption journey, and were now bringing bags to Guatemala for other parents in waiting. We all held a commonality of hope and a desire for connection with our children.

As we were greeted by the older children who were playing outside, my heart began to melt for each and every one of them. They stared at me with eyes of hope asking, "Are you my new family?" Instantaneously I wanted to pack them all in my suitcase and bring them home with me. My mom suggested a shopping cart. I told her she had the right idea. These children were old enough to understand, to a degree, what was happening. They filled me with light and sorrow at the same time. *All of this is so broken.*

When we returned to the hotel, I was handed a copy of our approval, which was basically a legal size piece of paper stating that AJ was ours. It was all in Spanish, as was our entire file, all 120 pages of it. I translated our approval into English using my new Spanish to

English and vice versa dictionary into the wee hours of the morning. I was much too excited to sleep.

Mom and I flew out of Guatemala on AJ's actual birthday. Our flight was due to land just after before midnight on the evening of the biggest fireworks show of the year. As we began our descent, I looked out over Lake Michigan to see the sky above it exploding with the annual fireworks for Milwaukee's music festival. "Happy Birthday AJ," I whispered. "Happy Birthday."

CHAPTER 6

No Stopping

When we figured out AJ wouldn't be home when we originally hoped, we lowered his crib mattress. After learning he still only weighed 13 pounds we raised the mattress again. I washed his crib set and put on a fresh new sheet. Daddy bought size one diapers. The toys we had received as shower gifts were opened and ready for little hands to explore. We started to wonder if the toy companies intentionally make the packing difficult to frustrate parents. *I think they do.* The car seat was installed in the back seat.

We had wrapped AJ in a stripped receiving blanket each time we visited him. *Red, blue, yellow.* I placed it in a re-sealable bag before we left Guatemala, trapping AJ's scent on the blanket. Each time we came home I placed the blanket in AJ's crib. Every day I would call our dogs into AJ's room, open the bag, and encourage them to sniff through the crib slates to get used to his scent. Our animals were preparing for our son's homecoming as well.

We completed our last bit of paperwork and started packing for our pick-up trip. I found myself thinking that whatever we didn't use for AJ we'd just stick in the bag for the orphanage. Old habits die hard.

We made our initial appointment with AJ's pediatrician. We had been communicating with her since we received AJ's referral, so she was as mutually excited about this meeting as we were. AJ's pediatrician was referred to us by one of Jeremy's colleagues. There was this constant butterfly feeling in both of our stomachs. *Was this really real? Nah, we're just going to visit him again…right?*

Less than month later I had a tiny window of time to make travel arrangements-as in, two days. In between booking airfares, our hotel, and securing a translator, we had started designing AJ's adoption announcements. A little bit of last-minute nesting did my heart good.

We were required to take custody of AJ on Friday, with our US Embassy appointment the following Monday. As a rule of safety, it was not recommended for adoptive parents to fly in or out of Guatemala at night. For the safety of your adopted child, tourist activities were encouraged to be experienced without your children. We searched for flights arriving Wednesday, leaving Thursday for tourism, and Friday for becoming parents. When you have a limited offer of travel times, you take what you can get.

After an entire day of travel, Jeremy and I arrived in Guatemala for the last time at around 10pm. The airport had been under construction for a while and this time we deplaned into the bright and shiny new terminal, totally disoriented. It was very late, and somehow I found myself missing the old squeaky luggage carousels in the old stuffy baggage claim area. Jeremy joined me in skating down the marble floors just as Mom had done with me just a month earlier.

Our regular taxi driver did not show. There we sat, in another new area of the Guatemalan airport without our regular driver. There were a hundred eager, grubby taxi drivers mustering up broken English to spit out cheap prices for cab fare. They reminded me of greasy vultures and made us very, very nervous.

We settled on a driver, who, out of all our choices, seemed to be the least scary. Along the way, I recognized where we were and tried to answer our driver's basic questions. Jeremy and I both felt a sense of calm when we when we turned onto the street where our hotel was located—until our driver made a right turn down a very dark alley.

He made another turn, this time left, which led down another dark alley which had a group of young men arguing, followed by a small pickup truck, with standard Guatemalan police decals, and very, very young men holding machine guns staring us down as we drove by. Our driver waved kindly as we passed by.

Panic-stricken, I once again turned to my broken Spanish and repeated "Casa Grande...derecha embajada de Estados Unidos" (to the right of the United States Embassy). I repeated it several times, even as he made another left and drove in front of a small building with charming adobe walls and slowed to a frightening low speed. "Casa Viaje," he announced. Again, I repeated my panicky sentence and suddenly it was clear. In my odd American accent, Casa Grande apparently meant Casa Viaje. He laughed and stepped on the gas, while he chanted "Casa Grande, a la derecha de la embajada de Estados Unidos!"

We finally arrived at the white gate at the front of our hotel, where I was ever thankful another taxi had arrived before us and the gate was already open and welcoming us. There was the gorgeous courtyard with its fountain that always brought me peace. We somehow crawled up to our room and collapsed.

We awoke the next morning rested and excited for our day trip to Antigua. It was not recommended to travel with your adopted children, so we purposely flew in the night before so we could spend the following day as tourists. Our trip to Antigua yielded nothing but absolute wonder. Our guide Francois spoke three languages, Spanish, English and French. He hosted an abundance of knowledge about Guatemala, its history, its present, and its future. I suppose this was his job, but even so, he was dazzling. As we drove toward the rural highway which led to Antigua, we stopped at a stoplight in a zone (Guatemala City is split into zones) where he announced, "This is a bad area."

I'm so glad we're stopped here.

He pointed out the locations of various crimes, all of which made me sick to my stomach, and praying the light would turn green. As we drove outside of the city, the road turned to freshly paved blacktop with bright yellow lines. Every telephone pole, every building, was littered with election flyers and advertisements. The stacked buildings soon turned into rich waves of beautiful green foliage. As we came up a rather steep hill, we began to see the presence of Guatemala's poverty. Shanty, corrugated aluminum sheds as houses, metal doors with small peek holes with slates as a sad attempt at safety. All I could think of was the price of corrugated aluminum and how readily available it is at the nearest home improvement store and how the uses greatly differed by country. As I listen to our tour guide explain Guatemala's history, I realized how this country's history has been a marriage between beauty and war.

We arrived on the outskirts of Antigua, when suddenly the smooth road turned into bumpity-bump-bump cobblestone roads. We opted out of the volcano tour, and turned our attention to the city itself. We wandered into Central Park, where the fountain of fertility stopped me in my tracks. She was beautiful, with water pouring out of her breasts as the giver of life. I felt ashamed and humbled at the same time. Francois told us women come to the fountain to pray for fertility or to thank her for their children. I quietly said a prayer for my own indirect fertility and for my son's birthmother. We toured ancient cathedrals and admired colonial architecture. We visited the Santa Domingo Monastery & Hotel where we stood mere feet from gorgeous parrots. We toured the Casa de Jade where I chose two jade pieces for AJ's godmothers. Being outside your element exposes such beauty and clarity. It is a mystery as to why we do not do this sort of thing more often.

We made our way to the rooftop of a former convent. I turned my attention below us to a gorgeous fountain in the open courtyard below us. It was star-shaped, but with so many points I lost count. It looked as though the water could reach every corner of the world. I didn't feel alone in this world, at all. I suddenly felt connected to everyone and everything around me. I wasn't alone. In this foreign country, where every single sense I possess was feeling something foreign, I felt alive and connected.

I slowly looked up and became awestruck by the view. Jeremy and I put our arms around each other and in that very moment, realized this was the last day of just Jeremy and Heidi. Tomorrow, we would become parents. While we already felt like parents, the fact remained that our house had not been blessed with the pitter-patter of little feet and the crib was empty. We embraced the moment without uttering any words.

As we walked through the streets, her face would stare back at me down every cobblestone road we walked on. Beautiful women, with coffee skin adorned with simplistic beauty. Every woman was a reflection of AJ's birthmother. I almost ran into one young girl who struck guilt in me. Guilt that was so deep I find most adjectives inadequate to describe it. She was a young teenager, with a beautiful sleeping baby in a wrap on her back. Our eyes met, and I turned away before she did. I had been struggling with the age similarity between myself and AJ's birthmother, together with the drastic differences in each of our lives, for quite some time. This young girl, was to me, the face of Guatemalan adoption. I simultaneously felt humbled, guilty, and awed all at the same time. I kept walking face down, full of pity and guilt, right down to my toes.

We entered a small open market where we were instantly bombarded by vendors. I felt compelled to buy one of everything. Our tour guide had given us such a great explanation of how this was how these people survived, that I felt ashamed to say no to any of them. A friend had told me about the baby wraps you could find at the market, and I set out to find one, hoping and praying just one would fit my well-endowed upper body. I turned the corner and stumbled upon a young mother breastfeeding her baby. Since baring your breast to breastfeed is a controversial topic here in the States I quickly looked away out of respect. But this mother engaged me and said "¡Hola!" with an honest smile.

I had noticed the baby was in a wrap, just like the ones I was looking to buy. I stammered through my weak Spanish and asked her about it. She turned and called for another female vendor and the two of them began conversing. They gave me two choices, two different patterns. I was fixed on this mother, who was working, with her baby on her breast, all the while smiling at me. She knew I was an adoptive Mom, buying this for the baby I was about to take out of her country, but yet, she kept smiling and feeding her baby. The women showed me how to tie the knot and slip it over my head. Not much to my surprise, it did not fit me and my boobs. I had wanted to buy one so badly, and felt even worse that these women had put forth extra effort and my body had said no for me.

As I was mulling it over, a little girl bounced out from under the mother's table. Jeremy came around the corner and seemed to sense my lack of comfort. We greeted the girl, I took one last look at the mother with her baby (still feeding), and quickly walked away. That was the end of our market shopping and the beginning of my tearful walk back to our guide.

How on earth can this be happening. My mind was stuck on repeat shuffle comparing my life to those of my Guatemalan counterparts. As we drove back toward the city, our tour guide suggested we stop in some of the villages outside of Antigua. All of them were "San Somethings." We drove into a village, where the first thing I spotted was a group of women smacking pieces of clothing against stone washboards. Francois chimed in with his explanation of what these women were doing and I felt my heart sink deeper and deeper into my chest.

This is not right.

We don't belong here.

They deserve better.

What can we do?

I want to run.

Did we want to get out of the car and walk around the square, he asked. No.

We drove around a few other villages, where we witnessed a children's marching band performing in the middle of the street along with a few mules and stray dogs running around. The band was entertaining, but two eyes caught my attention. A small girl was peeking through what I presumed was her front door; a rusted, steel panel in the middle of a crumbling house. A small hole had been cut into the door and covered with bars. Her eyes stared at me as our van was held up by the band. The night before I had been so excited to see the Starbucks coffee fields on the way back from Antigua. Suddenly, they didn't seem so grandiose anymore.

CHAPTER 7

Sharp Curve Ahead

Jeremy and I woke up entirely too early the next morning. We anxiously packed the gifts for the orphanage and made our way to the "couches of doom" to await our driver. Guatemalans run on something similar to island time, so we were not surprised when he was late picking us up. After 45 minutes of waiting, numerous phone calls began, back and forth between us, our attorney, and our driver. We lost our patience when were told we would not be "getting" AJ until around 5pm that evening. *Say what?* Apparently, he needed his physical and they were taking him to the hospital to the Embassy approved doctor. *Why hadn't this been done sooner?* I had a moment of sheer panic, thinking about what would happen if AJ didn't pass his physical. We would not be able to go to our Embassy appointment on Monday, he would not be granted a visa....

We waited...and waited...and waited. At 5pm I placed another phone call and was told they had just finished at the hospital and AJ would be dropped off soon. *Pardon?* We were told we would not be returning to the orphanage. I felt betrayed and angry I would not be able to see AJ in his first home one last time. We would not be able to say thank you to the staff, especially to Seina. I had envisioned crying and hugging her, sputtering "¡Gracías!" a hundred times as we embraced. I wanted to ask her tons of questions. I wanted to give her the bracelet I spent hours choosing for her and hand out the "mini-spa" bags another mom and I had put together for the entire staff. We deserved that closure. *Didn't we?*

A few moments later, a car pulled up and two caregivers got out of the car. With the exception of the sunshine and gentle movement of the caregivers, it reminded me of a scene from an old gangster movie. I had not noticed AJ sleeping in one of the girl's arms until they were all in front of me. She placed him in my arms...FOREVER. He stayed sleeping as we were handed an envelope.

Envelope?

That's it?

We had been warned that even though we sent a disposable camera it would only be by chance we'd get it back. They began to leave! I screamed, motioning to the large bag of gifts that was sitting on the couch. They offered a curt response of thank you and then they were gone.

He was dressed in a white and blue onesie, a long-sleeved fall-themed onesie, khaki pants, and socks. He was dripping with sweat, of course, and continued to do so as he slept. We took a moment to enjoy what God had just given us and stared at him in awe. Bliss.

Another adoptive father approached us quietly and whispered congratulations along with "this is your moment" as he walked away. Little did we know that moment would be our only moment of true bliss for a very long time.

We made our way upstairs to our room where he woke up. We stripped him down to his lighter onesie and fed him. He downed 6 ounces like a champ. We sat him up, only to discover he could only "tripod". He stayed upright for about 10 seconds before he tipped over like a teapot. He was able to grasp objects and follow things with his eyes...especially his bottle when it was all gone. He held his head up higher than he had just a month ago. We were sure he would be army crawling in a week or two at most. We spent a while trying to get AJ used to a spoon in and around his mouth. It did not come as a surprise that he was still not on solid foods. We spent the rest of the evening playing with AJ and looking over his gargantuan envelope of paperwork.

We spent Saturday hanging out around the hotel and watching AJ sleep and eat. He was sick again with a cough that kept him pretty worn out and sleepy. Jeremy gave him a bath and I suddenly noticed how long his body was, yet his belly was round and protruding.

Something to talk to his pediatrician about.

AJ began to show signs of stress, which was expected. All children that are adopted go through a period of grieving, and as hard as it was to watch, we knew, or thought it would pass.

On Monday morning we had our US Embassy appointment bright and early. For his very important day, AJ sported a nautical short and sweater set and his first pair of shoes that actually fit. He slept almost the entire time we were at the embassy. Think of it as the

DMV, only three times as crowded and loud and with babies. Our translator was a sweetheart and walked us through every step of the morning. *Stand up, sit down, stand up, sit down.* At the end of our appointment, we were given the information that the US Embassy physician had written about AJ..."some developmental delays, follow-up with primary care physician" and told us to come back the next day. It sounded simple enough and we felt prepared.

Jeremy returned from the Embassy the next morning with a huge grin on his face, along with AJ's VISA and the packet that was to be hand carried to our port of entry into the US and given to immigration. We spent the day hanging out, taking pictures and did our best to soak it all in. It was becoming increasingly clear that AJ was sick, and most definitely developmentally delayed. We were glad that we'd be on our way home in 15 hours, but my heart was also aching for my son. He was about to lose everything he had known, permanently. *Permanently.*

CHAPTER 8

Detour

We climbed into our taxi to the Guatemalan airport. My heart was as heavy as my suitcase. While we were elated to bring AJ home, I was hounded with guilt that I was taking our baby boy away from his homeland. I cried all the way to the airport, quickly wiping my tears as we pulled up. I sobbed carrying him down the pristine glass jet-way as we boarded our flight. Our flight to Houston was uneventful, except for AJ's discomfort and screaming while we were in our final descent. The flight attendant gave me a gentle yet firm speech, telling me I should give him a bottle during both ascent and descent. I felt like punching her. I may be a new parent, but I am well prepared, sister. *I know that lady, but what am I supposed to do if he doesn't want it?! I followed all of the suggestions given to me, ma'am, and none of them worked... now back off.*

As we walked to the terminal, I snapped at Jeremy. I took my sheer anger toward the flight attendant and unleashed on my husband instead. This was the first of many times I would snap at Jeremy out of fear and nerves. I was so glad to be in on American soil, yet knew we had so far to go and I sensed something was going on. I didn't know what, but I felt it. After a long period that felt like detainment in the Immigration and Customs office, we were called to the counter and again encouraged to have AJ see his pediatrician based on the embassy physician's note. *Alright people, we get it. We're responsible parents. His appointment is the day after we arrive home. Now back off!*

We were greeted by Jeremy's cousin and his family at the baggage claim. Marty and Michele had provided steadfast support during our adoption process. These two were always quick with hospitality and slow with goodbyes. What a relief to see familiar faces! As we drove toward their home for the evening, my stress level sky-rocketed. *What is wrong with me?* Michele noticed and made a quick call, requesting pizza and margaritas to be waiting when we arrived. As always, we were presented with true Southern hospitality, complete with a pack and play and a basket full of gifts and supplies for AJ.

We enjoyed a quiet evening with Jeremy's family and experienced confirmation that AJ was definitely sick. He was up multiple times during the night for bottles and was just restless. I spent most of the night in the den watching sports, since I couldn't figure out how to change the channel. I was instantly in mom mode, knowing something wasn't quite right, knowing when he'd want a bottle, with my anxiety to get home increasing by the second. For some reason, I had serious nerves battling my conscious about the plane ride home.

When we woke up the next day, my nerves had increased. *Massively.* As we drove to the airport, I was shaking and crying uncontrollably in the backseat. Michele had given me 1,258 pep talks and continued to do so until the moment we were walking into the airport. I hugged her and thanked her. Sending flowers following our visit was never enough of a thank you to this fellow adoptive momma who took this terrified new mother under her wing.

In the airport, my nerves calmed. AJ fell asleep on the airport floor and people found him so adorable.

Why does he sleep with his body all cock-eyed?

We managed to secure the bulk head seats for the flight.

Thank you to the couple who generously gave up their seats for the young couple with their new baby from Guatemala.

Twenty minutes into the flight, we were cruising at an altitude of a violently ill baby. AJ suddenly shook his entire body and projectile vomited through his mouth and nose, all over me. I have never, till this day, seen a child throw up with that much force. Thank God for the loud roar of the plane. The only person who noticed he wasn't well was the lady across the aisle from us, and the kind and helpful male flight attendant. *While I know he was trying to be helpful, paper napkins don't do much honey. Ok? Ok.*

AJ continued throwing up every few minutes. Jeremy became concerned about the possibility of choking, because he was flipping his head backwards while vomiting. *I was thanking my stars Jeremy had chosen to become a nurse.* I ran AJ down the airplane aisle to the bathroom and held him over the sink. Nothing.

I returned to our seats and we prayed, prayed harder than either of us had ever prayed in our entire lives, that AJ would fall asleep. He did. Jeremy fed me a sandwich as AJ slept on my shoulder. Slow tears escaped down my cheeks. "I want to go home", I cried.

We landed and I was thankful AJ was still sleeping. As we walked up the jetway, I could feel AJ's body begin to shake like a little volcano. *Jesus make this STOP. Somebody make this STOP.* I started to increase my stride. By the time I reached the terminal door I was running with this limp volcanic child in my arms, ready to explode at any time. I ran to the family bathroom which was occupied. There was no other bathroom in sight. I held him to my chest while he got sick again. Jeremy caught up with me and joined me in extreme irritation as a businessman walked out of the family bathroom.

Once vacant, we ran into the bathroom and began the panic dance. I stripped AJ down and changed his clothes, Jeremy took off his vomit soaked jacket and called the nurses line for our pediatrician's office. No answer. Our plane had come in delayed, therefore after business hours. He called the after-hours line and left a message, which was oh so helpful. AJ was limp, lethargic, and beyond HOT. I took off my vomit soaked sweater and we finally tromped up the terminal to meet our family and friends.

AJ was a lump on my shoulder as we introduced him to our family and friends. Just as all grandmothers do, my Grandma ignored my warnings about him being sick and insisted on holding him for just a moment. I only remember these things after viewing a short video that was taken. My brain was so not concentrated on hugging people or receiving congratulations.

This was not the way it was supposed to be.

At some point we found ourselves walking in the parking structure to find our car. *Safe and sound and on our way home. So we thought.* As we pulled out of the parking structure, I heard a gurgling sound from the backseat. I completely turned around and saw that AJ was vomiting again. I felt him to see if he had a fever. I have never felt a child so HOT. I told Jeremy to choose between urgent care and the hospital and drive. He drove warp speed to the urgent care office where one of his colleagues happened to be on as the urgent-care doctor. Our sweet baby boy had double ear infections, an upper respiratory infection, and a fever of 102. No wonder he was violently ill. No wonder he didn't do well on the plane rides. *No wonder.*

In just a diaper, we put AJ in his car seat and finally headed home. We drove up to an empty house. *Not comforting after the last few hours. None of this was how it was supposed to be.*

Jeremy carried him in the house and held him on his shoulder in our dining room. How many times had I pictured our sweet boy home? Nothing I could have imagined would have been sweeter than that precious moment. He needed us, we needed him. We had come full circle and it felt good and nauseating to be home.

Couch. Takeout. Mail. Normalcy.

The dogs welcomed AJ with lots of sniffs and kisses, as if he already belonged here. Rocky, our German Shepherd, patrolled as I bathed AJ in the bathroom sink. *This is the second time I am bathing my baby in a bathroom sink. He's not supposed to be this small.* He sucked his first bottle at home dry and fell asleep almost instantly as I laid him in his crib. Rocky continued on patrol all night. *AJ is his baby.* I stood watching my sweet baby sleep. At home. Finally. *Welcome home baby boy. Welcome Home.*

CHAPTER 9

New Signal Ahead

AJ's first few days home were a bit of a red carpet event, complete with Mommy paparazzi. We took him to his first pediatric appointment, where we learned AJ was severely malnutritioned. I remembered our last night in Guatemala where Jeremy gave AJ a bath. His body was long and thin, with a distended belly. He looked like those children you see on the child hunger infomercials. *I shudder even now when I look at that picture.* His tone was low, which was expected, and we switched him from formula to Pediasure. He had only been fed formula for those 13 months and weighed just 13 pounds. We were to start him on baby solid foods and cereal immediately. He endured a slew of lab tests. This was the first and last time they did a heel prick on my child. *Mercy.* When we had walked into the lab, Jeremy had gone green and excused himself when the technician came in to draw what seemed like all of AJ's blood. *Weird.* When we finished with our appointment, we went upstairs to greet Jeremy's co-workers and introduce our new little bundle of joy. They surprised us with a huge cake and gifts for AJ.

Oh, he's so tiny!

AJ took quite well to his exersaucer and learned quickly to bang his toys around on the tray. He mastered rice cereal and bananas in no time at all. We began working his legs with his play mat, which led to lots of tummy time and AJ feeling carpet for the first time. Five days after arriving home AJ had gained four ounces. He had no problem eating whatsoever and slept through anything and everything....

He hated green beans, but loved sweet potatoes, pears, bananas, and carrots. He preferred tummy time to being on his back. We introduced him to a walker. At his two-week follow up at the pediatrician AJ had gained over a pound. Our pediatrician was thrilled with his progress, as his head circumference and length had also increased. His muscle tone had improved as well, and she was confident it would continue to do so with physical therapy. He learned to completely turn himself around in the exersaucer and started shaking his head from side to side over and over. It was rather strange. He began to roll much more efficiently and was convinced that if he yelled at a toy it would come to him. *The boy channeled Harry Potter from a young age.*

Prior to our pick-up trip we had contacted our county's Birth to 3 Early Intervention program. We knew AJ would need some physical and occupational therapy so we planned ahead to begin services as soon as possible. A young fresh-faced social worker walked in our door and while she was oohing and aahing over AJ, I was pushing for information as to when we could get started. *Time is of the essence here lady.* She was rather passive in her answers and promised to set up evaluations for AJ in the coming weeks.

A physical and an occupational therapist came to the house a week or so later to complete evaluations on AJ. Other than asking me questions and all my answers being no or I don't know, both therapists were rather quite during their time here until the PT stated AJ was at a one-month-old level. Instantly, I decided I didn't like her. *What on earth was she talking about?!* The OT put her finger in the palm of AJ's left hand and he screamed bloody murder. Nothing would soothe him except the swing. *What on earth?* They both agreed he needed therapy and asked if twice a week would work for us. I numbly said yes and held my anger as they walked out my front door. I called Jeremy in tears. How could he be at a one-month-old level? *Morons.* He agreed with me, that these people must be insane, and we left it at that.

AJ graduated to size two diapers and 6-9 month sleepers in just a month at home. Despite his growth, he had gained a very small amount of weight which alarmed his pediatrician, as he had been gaining steadily over the last few weeks. He stood against an object and supported his own weight for the first time and moved on to a seated bath chair. He loved water and figured out he could move the water with his hands and feet. I was witnessing beauty daily as he began to come out of his shell and use his body. *This is good. Things are going well. We can do this.*

We started to feel anxious about beginning his therapies. AJ's appointment at our hospital's Child Development Center did not help. As he was sitting on my lap, the development specialist placed countless objects on the table...I held my breath when he rang the bell.

Jeremy and I had suspected some type of hearing loss during our final days in Guatemala. *I bet he's just used to "orphanage noise" and is ignoring us.* We had done the *Mr. Holland's Opus* thing, dropping pots on the floor kitchen floor. We were not surprised by his lack of reaction. We pushed to have his hearing tested as soon as possible. *Push. Demand. Same thing.*

Besides the bell ringing ordeal, AJ was diagnosed with global developmental delay. We were already on the fast track to therapies, and getting all of our suspicions "checked out". It was the first of many appointments where they'd tell us to just keep doing what we were already doing. I thought that was a strange statement.

Our next appointment was for the ophthalmology clinic. I felt like such a rookie at the hospital and in that particular clinic. While I was finally relieved to get him for all of these appointments, because that meant AJ was here and not in Guatemala, I was still a new mom suddenly thrust into appointments with doctors with titles I couldn't spell correctly on the first try.

There are two h's in ophth....

The ophthalmologist seemed to take forever to see us, and when she did, she didn't have good news. AJ had bilateral esotropia; crossing of the eyes. Thankfully, they crossed at different times, which was a good thing. We would try patching, but were told AJ would need corrective eye surgery. Our placement agency had told us about AJ's eyes, so this came as no surprise.

We began hosting physical, occupational, and early education therapists every week in our home. It was love at first sight for AJ and the yoga ball we used for his exercises. He was more in tune with his body. After a month home, he army crawled into our hallway. This was his first solo adventure outside of the living room. While he made steady progress, his therapists as well as his pediatrician all suggested AJ see a neurologist. *A neurologist? They did a brain scan in Guatemala. It was fine. What are they not telling me?!*

AJ's baptism was in October. I had asked my Mom to create a baptismal outfit for AJ from my wedding dress, her wedding dress, and my mother-in-law's wedding dress. She graciously agreed, and the result was nothing short of humbling. AJ just made it through church and was presented to the congregation, as all children are, with the pastor walking up and down the center aisle with our boy.

As we began taking pictures, random people called out AJ's name. He did not respond. As we posed for pictures, both Jeremy and I sang, through gritted smiling teeth, *"He can't hear you"*. As AJ commenced his meltdown, we left. We had not publicly shared our suspicious about his hearing loss yet. Slowly his delays were becoming more noticeable to both of us.

I took him to the audiology clinic to have his hearing checked. He did not respond to anything. They used some type of gun/price scanner looking thing, with a probe on the end of it, which yielded no reading whatsoever. This made them move us to another room where they put probes in ears and then told me it was probably just fluid in his ears. We were referred to an ENT. An ENT that was not a pediatric ENT, he was a regular ENT who was, again, old school. *I'm a new mom, what do I know? He came highly recommended.* As he had his staff cocoon wrap AJ on a flat board, I watched as he did not respond to my soothing voice and screamed uncontrollably. Tears, just as uncontrollable flowed down his tiny little cheeks and I knew, just knew, this wasn't the last time we'd be in this predicament.

The ENT recommended ear tubes for AJ, so the simple procedure was scheduled at an outpatient surgical center. It was unclear at that point as to what AJ could hear. We did know that he was not hearing normal speech or normal environmental sounds like the TV, phone, or water running. We thought he was hearing our huge Labrador's bark.

On an early weekday morning, Jeremy prepared to leave for work with a very angry wife in his face. What do you mean you aren't coming with me to the outpatient surgery center? What DO YOU MEAN? Jeremy and had already begun his retreat from all things AJ and this was another step down the road to elsewhere. He finally obliged and accompanied us.

The facility was not prepared, nor familiar with procedures on such a small child. They weighed him by me holding him and stepping on a scale. After the procedure, the ENT came out and shared there was a complication during the procedure. "Your son's airway tried to close. He's floppy; you should take him to a neurologist".

I'm sorry. What! *What did you just say?!*

AJ was in so much pain he stopped breathing for short periods of time. You know, that hold your breath because it hurts so badly with the delayed cry? That. To the degree he his oxygen level dropped enough for these outpatient surgery center staff members to freak out.

With the tubes in place, another hearing test was scheduled. I vowed to never return to that doctor.

Shortly after his surgery, we put on our happy faces and hosted AJ's Welcome Home Fiesta at our church. Everyone welcomed AJ home with open arms and swooned over his delicate yet handsome features. The eyelashes people would kill for. The sheen of his silky black hair. His adorable smile and oh-so pinchable cheeks.

Jeremy and I saw the differences between AJ and the other kids at the party immediately. We introduced his new therapists and gushed over them. Sometime between our initial meeting and the party I had decided they knew what they were talking about and began to soak up everything I could to help AJ. We knew he couldn't hear. We knew he couldn't see. Inside, we were crumbling and terrified to know what was next.

CHAPTER 10

Danger Ahead

It took me almost four months to come clean with our family and friends as to *everything* that what was really going on with AJ. We had a website that eventually morphed into a blog, but I was never able to be honest about the torment our hearts were feeling or the fear that was all consuming. Our journey was supposed to be over. *Over.* We were supposed to be beginning a new journey of actual parenting. Those journeys were quite different in our eyes. Well, at least they had been.

AJ was diagnosed with failure to thrive during his third pediatrician appointment. He was not gaining weight or growing as fast as his pediatrician would have liked him to given all of these extra calories he was getting. We were referred to a gastroenterologist, who felt he was doing well enough to continue a high-calorie intake, only instead of Pediasure; we were allowed to give him whole milk with Carnation Instant Breakfast mixed in. *Much cheaper.* He continued to scarf down Stage 3 chunky baby foods and began on soft people foods.

AJ's left side soon began to "lag". We started to notice he was slouching to the left and not using his left hand but instead fisting.

This was causing major concern, so we pushed to have an MRI of his brain done. We were encouraged to have our pediatrician order the MRI instead of the neurologist. We did just that. That appointment had me terrified. A young, handsome anesthesiologist came in and listened to our experience with the ear tube procedure. AJ was given Versed, or as I call it "joy juice", and began to relax. Soon, the anesthesiologist was carrying my boy down the hall to the elevator and to the MRI room. He made sure AJ had his beloved rainbow koosh ball before they entered the room and I paced in the hallway. I was beyond thankful he allowed me to just wait in the hallway. He could see my fear, my worry.

They came out much sooner than expected and he was holding my little man in his arms again. The team had decided not to put him under. The anesthesiologist had decided to simply stand next to him and talk to him in an effort to keep him calm. He shared with me his discovery of AJ's past. Gently lifting his hand, he showed me the scars of my son's past. Tiny scars on my baby's hand from entirely too many IV's. The female staff members all came out to squeal and fawn over my little lover boy. He's a ladies man, this I know. I was both in shock and relieved that the anesthesiologist had chosen to do the scan without a sedative.

A few days later we received the results, revealing AJ did have an abnormality of the brain.

Periventricular leukomalacia.

Periventricular leukomalacia.

The report read "non-specific" change…that happened perinatal or during delivery. It was a question as to whether his delays were caused solely by his brain damage and/or orphanage delay. We would not find out any straight answers until his appointment with the neurologist in December. *December.* AJ had accomplished three months-worth of therapy in one month, which was a good sign.

We were anxious about AJ's upcoming hearing test, called an ABR-Auditory Brainstem Response. After intense fighting with our early intervention program, AJ was finally granted a speech evaluation, followed by speech therapy at least twice a week. Our program originally said their early education specialist could do the speech evaluation. I said no. After just two visits, I could see that this was not working. AJ had some sort of hearing loss and playing "coochie-coochie cooo" on his changing table was not cutting it. We pushed for speech therapy for the obvious reasons, but also for feeding and overall oral motor control.

AJ had never tolerated "hard" things anywhere near his mouth. From baby spoons to cheerios, it wasn't happening. We sat on the floor of a very experienced feeding specialist's office and I learned of his oral aversions. After a few sessions of rubbing his lips with crushed shortbread cookies, AJ opened his mouth to explore what his speech therapist had on her hand. A few days later, he grabbed a piece of turkey off the Thanksgiving table to "explore".

Perhaps what held up our desperation for hope was AJ's reaction to all that was going on around him. He was so oblivious. Despite all that he was going through, he was a happy little man. *Maybe all of these professionals are wrong. He's happy. He'll get there. It will be fine.*

We thought we had fought our last fight with the early intervention program and the hospital. No more red tape. We thought we were finally settling in. We were finally getting answers and getting treatment for our son. The land of unknown was scary. Our first holiday home with our son was much to be thankful for, but oh so clouded with fear.

CHAPTER 11

Crash

The weather following our beautiful Thanksgiving was gloomy and unwelcomed. Mother Nature was giving us that hazy mix of fall and winter that falls in the form of freezing cold rain that feels wetter than water. It didn't help our moods of uncertainty.

I drove to the hospital for AJ's ABR test and sat in the cold, dark day-surgery room, keeping him entertained while we waited. The nurse came in with the "joy juice" and my sweet boy relaxed. The audiologist came in and explained the test to me. How he'd be sedated, how the equipment would send sounds and how they'd see where he responded. This audiologist was not the original one we saw for his initial hearing test. I was annoyed.

I called my Mom, who was at the hospital with my Dad. He was in the midst of battling his second round of cancer and was in the hospital for a heart issue. I told my Mom AJ was being tested. The window was fogging with my breathing as I looked out over a parking lot. My Dad came on the line and told me he'd be home in a few days. I told him where AJ was and that I was scared. He told me, "Everything's going to be fine." I felt peace in his words and wished I could split myself in two and be there for him and my mom as well as my own son.

Jeremy and I had fought that morning. I don't recall what it was about but it didn't matter the moment he walked through the door in our day surgery suite. AJ was already gone when he arrived. I kept staring at the silver paper towel holder next to the sink, thinking this was a time for reflection; both literally and figuratively.

The moment we saw the audiologist coming towards us we became a unified front. She approached us slowly:

"We didn't get much response at all."

What does that mean?

"We tested to the maximum lowest level the machine goes and he did not respond."

What does that mean?

"So what can he hear?" we asked.

"Not much, maybe a jet engine." His loss is profound. The equipment tests to 110dB, he did not respond."

A jet engine? What does profound mean? What is dB?

If I just keep staring at her she'll say something different. The rest of what she said sounded *like blah, blah, blah, blah, blah. Big words, big words, beat around the bush.*

We were NOT expecting to learn that our son was DEAF.

Completely. Deaf.

We booth stood in shock. We thought he could at least hear **something**. The audiologist was trying to be so gentle with us. I wondered what type of training she had been given on giving parents such devastating news. After all the red tape with his adoption and just getting him the required appointments and tests, we just wanted answers.

She said we'd trial hearing aids, but children with his degree of loss typically do not respond to hearing aids. She mentioned the words cochlear implants. *Huh?* I drove home in the cold rain, sobbing. *Swish. Swish.* My tears were falling as the rain was sloshed by my windshield wipers. *Why is this happening?*

The next day AJ and I went to the hospital to visit my Dad. It was my first time up at bat with the "my son has _____" cadence. I had to look my family in the eye and tell them my son was deaf.

The flood of questions began.

"Well how deaf?"

"I mean he can hear something, can't he?"

They stared at him like he was some kind of alien.

I wanted to run.

FAR.

Can't you just look at AJ and see AJ?

No.

Suddenly he had a neon sign blinking "deaf" on his forehead.

My Dad was in and out of it and I knew. He stared at me with these eyes, like he was trying to ingrain the image of my face and AJ's in his mind—forever. I knew, in that moment, he was leaving us. His story had changed from having a heart issue with discharge in a few days to a pulmonary embolism to multiple clots in his lung. He was only expected to live through the weekend.

The next evening I rushed to the hospital after my Mom had called and told me it was time. I hugged my Mom as she assured me she'd be fine.

I wanted to take her pain-she wanted to take mine.

As I turned to walk out, I saw my Mom in the recliner next to my Dad, holding his hand, soothing his tired soul and encouraging him to let go. In that moment, I prayed that I would be strong enough to possess that much strength at some point in my lifetime.

The next morning we saw AJ's neurologist. We had pushed and pushed and pushed to have his MRI done sooner than later. AJ was diagnosed with cerebral palsy. The diagnosis was not a shock, but the generality of it was. He was not able to tell us if AJ would walk, talk, or function like you and I do. He told us to keep doing what we were doing, as we were already involved in all of the resources he was going to suggest.

I called my mom on the way home and told her AJ had cerebral palsy. I can still hear the sound of the wipers on the car I was driving sludging the rain back and forth as I told her.

Half an hour later, as I was laying AJ down for a nap, the phone rang.

And I knew.

Dad was gone.

I crumbled at the thought that I could not be there for my own Mother.

How was this happening? How in the world were we supposed to process all of this, ***period***, much less all at the same time?

Dad's funeral was a blur. What I remember most is staring blankly into people's eyes as they shared their sympathies with me. Not once, but twice; once for my father, and once for my son. I was way too numb to process any of it.

Christmas came and went. I look back on pictures from that Christmas and see two parents with two broken hearts. Broken hearts that could not be put back together, no matter how much tape or glue was applied.

We soon learned that AJ gives hope in the worst of times. He crawled a week after Christmas and began holding his own bottle in a seated position. He experienced snow and cold, cold weather. Giving hope in the midst of darkness was the gift my child was given.

CHAPTER 12

Road Conditions

AJ's disabilities began to open up a whole new world for not only him, but for us as parents. I was a sponge eager to learn anything and everything I could to help AJ. While I fought insurance for services, AJ made more gains. We began to learn what worked for AJ, and what didn't work. Large crowds, forced sitting or being still sent his sensory system into overload. We began to encounter people who were not so kind about AJ's disabilities and their reactions to his disabilities brought out some fierce reactions from me. My heart would thump in frustration and anger; frustration toward AJ's disabilities and anger towards strangers who just didn't get it. In addition to his major and more well-known diagnoses, he had severe sensory processing disorder.

AJ's hearing aids indeed did not benefit him. We had grieved and processed our son's hearing loss and were overly anxious to move forward toward cochlear implants. The process of cochlear implant candidacy was daunting, especially with a child who didn't have the best ability to respond as a typically developing child would. Cochlear implant candidacy is no joke. In fact a letter to our senator was necessary to force the powers that be to make an eligibility determination. My grandmother always said I should have been a lawyer. I never back down from a fight.

When it came to AJ, I fought harder.

After his hearing loss diagnosis we were referred to our local center for hearing and deafness. A Teacher of the Deaf came out to our home and did an evaluation. She brought "the chart". The chart that lists the different communication modes for deaf children.

Choose your path.

Here. Now.

We knew we were going to pursue cochlear implants. We had no idea of knowing if they would work, how they would work, how he would respond, or what his future held. We knew this would be challenging, no matter what route we chose.

We chose total communication as a means to give AJ a way to communication without amplification and help bridge the transition from no sound to sound. We knew teaching him ASL (American Sign Language) would be difficult with his limited fine motor abilities and limited spatial awareness. Total communication combines spoken language with sign language. The sign language is English based, or what we referred to as C.A.S.E., Conceptually Accurate Signed English. After discussing this at length with his Teacher of the Deaf, we made the choice. She began to teach both us and AJ basic signs and gave us homework each and every week to help our little man learn.

I love homework.

AJ was most successful with signing for food. His first sign was the word more. It is not shocking that the "boy who eats everything and then some" signed more as his first word. His feeding skills also began to increase. He learned to scoop foods with a spoon and drink from a sippy cup. His cognitive gains began to explode. He began eating with a fork. His journey could be described as he began, he began, he began….

When he began learning to walk, we found ourselves in for a long haul. Imagine sitting in a neurologist's office, having a doctor tell you he's not sure if your son will walk.

How can you, the specialist, not know? Don't you know all the things about all the things?

I had softened my opinion of his therapists, specifically his physical therapist. You know, the one I called a moron? In fact, she became AJ's biggest asset, cheerleader, and coach.

Well, besides his parents.

I had learned her background and fell in love with her teaching style. I got past my emotions and focused on the goal. I was hungry and eager to learn and help AJ any way I could. She kept assuring us HE WILL WALK.

HE WILL WALK.

WITHOUT BRACES.

WITHOUT CANES.

WITHOUT A WALKER.

HE WILL WALK.

And he did.

Practice makes a milestone.

We spent six months teaching him to bear his own full weight, balance, move while balancing, and stop. With his physical therapist's support, I never thought anything other than he will walk. I look back to videos we shot when he was learning to walk. He doesn't even look like the same child. No body awareness, no balance, no ability to catch himself on the way down. Holding tight to the mindset of his future (without metal or wheels) gave us focus and determination.

AJ's mobility clashed with his cerebral palsy. Children with cerebral palsy burn calories twice as fast. We increased AJ's calorie intake as he became more active. His appetite was vivacious. We were feeding him things we never thought we'd feed our child. I wanted so badly to be a pita bread and hummus mother. And then his gastroenterologist explained that he could literally eat frozen custard for every meal because he was that underweight.

At age 2 years 9 months, Jeremy and I found ourselves sitting in the surgery waiting area as AJ underwent surgery for his first cochlear implant. After almost an entire year of booth testing, a psychological evaluation, and consultations, here we were. The audiologist called the surgery waiting room and said, "AJ is hearing".

I told her to shut up.

Yes, in the middle of a packed waiting room, I yelled "Shut Up!" into the phone.

When I was finally called back to the recovery area, I was not prepared for what I was about to experience. AJ was in such intense pain he would stop breathing and holding his breath. The nurse asked if I was ok, and I nodded, semi-aware of what was happening. I stood helpless. His oxygen level was dropping and he needed to cry, and most importantly breathe.

We felt 100% sure this was the right decision, but my heart was crying out for my baby boy's pain to cease. After a good dose of pain medication, he relaxed in my arms.

That night in the hospital was not for the novice. I sat on the uncomfortable rocker-turns-into-an-uncomfortable bed for a few hours, praying he would stay sleeping.

They say when you get older, you wish for your parents to be there in difficult moments; just as they were there for the boo-boo's and colds that required chicken soup. Adults are supposed to handle the hard stuff, aren't we? Never have I wanted my own mother more.

Jeremy was at home and I was alone.

Adrenaline was curbing the tears and forcing the pragmatic side of me to function. AJ would wake up, vomiting blood and I would begin to clean him and his bed as I hit the button for the nurse. We'd finish changing him and she'd give him a dose of medications, and I'd fall into that recliner again. The next morning Jeremy came in with my favorite coffee shop concoction and we were itching to go home. We fought with the resident on AJ's case, insisting he needed a different anti-nausea medication. Indeed he did, it was given, and he was miraculously our happy boy again.

Two days after his surgery we landed in the hospital as I couldn't get him to keep anything down. We waited four hours in a tiny room off the main waiting area as my son vomited into my chest with an open wound (stitches) on his head. He was given fluids and we were sent home.

What on earth was that?

This was the first of many times we'd ponder that question.

AJ began attending a toddler group for deaf children using total communication. His cochlear implant activation was amazing. While it did not bring the sudden, typical results we had silently hoped for (and watched on YouTube), we knew his experience, and that every child's experience is different.

We still had hope.

AJ struggled in his toddler group. Most days I prayed he'd make it through the first ten minutes of circle time. Usually his limbs were flailing and I was trying to keep my cool. I'd sit behind the glass and watch him enjoy snack time but disregard most of the rest of his time with his peers. It was this time that I savored and hated simultaneously. The gap between my son and his peers was staggering and so difficult to swallow.

I had been given the miraculous ability to separate my son's issues from him and process them compartmentalized.

Child over here, issues over here.

It was survival.

We transitioned from our early intervention program and the toddler group into preschool. We had researched and found an amazing cochlear implant preschool program an hour away. As I took webinars and other preparation classes for entering your special needs child into the public school system, I soaked up everything I could to be the best advocate for AJ.

We had our first IEP (Individual Education Plan) for AJ just after he turned three. I still remember the four table's worth of people who were there, and where they sat. I had made binders for each and every person explaining who AJ was, sharing pictures, his strengths and weaknesses, our desires for him as his parents, and supporting documentation as to why he needed to attend another school in a neighboring district. The meeting lasted over three hours and ended with no solid conclusion. A few weeks later we proved this was the best option for AJ and our home district contracted for him to attend in the neighboring district.

He succeeded in that preschool.

We continued to work on feeding. We continued all therapies. I learned what decreased oral-awareness meant. We moved on to stairs and climbing. We worked on fine-motor skills and greater, functional use of his left extremities. I sought out every sensory toy I could find to fill his need for sensory experiences. We painted with pudding and made rice treats. We painted with our feet and took him to aqua therapy, hippotherapy, and tried to parallel the work they were doing at school here at home.

AJ received his second cochlear implant a year after his first. He was discharged from physical therapy at age five. FIVE. He learned to drink from a straw, a cup, and bottles (water not formula). He moved from never having solids to only having one food on the "no" list. He has defied his odds over and over. He endured his mother's insatiable love for cute pictures. He learned to hold his breath underwater. He DEFIED.

I could go on, and on, and on. But here is where the story shifts.

NARROW BRIDGE

When this book was in the final stages of edits I was given the suggestion that the beginning was very linear with the second half reading very reflective. I could banter on listing AJ's milestones one by one throughout his almost ten years on this earth. But the truth is I want to share more than listing AJ's milestones. I want to share my experience as a mother.

Through this writing process I have learned that both my brain and my heart have narrowed the early days of my journey through motherhood. Perhaps there is a Pandora's box of emotions waiting out there somewhere that just shouldn't be opened. As hard as I have tried, I have not been successful with tapping into that period of my life and being reflective. It is all very linear and factual in my brain and in my heart. Perhaps we point to this period in my life as survival mode. I can give you the factual, operation response with a few emotions sprinkled in, but that's about it.

I like to think of this as a success; a huge success actually. A tremendous amount of healing has occurred since Chapter 1 of this journey. I'd like to keep moving forward…

CHAPTER 13

Learning Curve

It was the night AJ had been diagnosed deaf. It was still raining; streaking down the picture window in our living room as I hauled out this big binder they had given us just hours earlier. This was the first moment I remember really diving into this type of information. Of course we had been given information before that moment, but this was the moment I felt like I was drowning. From the instant I opened this binder I felt someone holding me under water, refusing to allow me air. The whole room was sucked of oxygen. I was reading, but not retaining. I was reading aloud to Jeremy, but he was staring at the wall. The binder, in its soft pastels and smiling pictures could not change the chemistry of my broken heart. The information was helpful, but still cold; initiated by parents of deaf children, but still stale. Quotes from these parents offered a sliver of hope, but I still found myself unable to relate to them. I read through the entire binder, and then stored it in a closet for years. It was never opened again until I burned the binder itself and its contents in a ceremonial fire of release.

Sometimes you just cannot retain the facts, much less process them.

It takes time to assemble your armor and become the advocate you want to be for your child.

Over the years the information we have researched and received has evolved. It has been critical, necessary, and provided quite a learning curve. A few years before AJ's adoption I had completed an Associate Degree as a medical administrative specialist. I had taken classes such as medical terminology, billing, coding, and transcription. While I was unsure as to where this degree was going to lead me professionally, I certainly hold a firm understanding now as to why I obtained that degree. It was my first exposure to the world of medical terms, understanding insurance benefits and claims. It gave me confidence when I began calling insurance companies and navigating AJ's ever increasing number of specialists. I knew what EOB, DOS, FU, and CMP meant. Big words and long terms for specific specialists did not scare me. I knew how to spell gastroenterologist before he was added to AJ's medical team. My learning curve continued to increase as AJ's multiple disabilities meant an enormous amount of information to learn and retain.

I said I love homework.

We skipped straight to binders. Binders of specialists with fun colored dividers to provide me with some fun in the midst of matter-of-fact. All of this learning molded the term advocate. I still struggle with this term. I much prefer the active term of advocating. The learning has yet to cease. I may feel well-versed in the worlds of hemiplegic cerebral palsy, bilateral profound hearing loss, and partial epilepsy, but don't let that fool you. As he learns, I learn. His landscape has changed more times than I can count. Keeping him on the straight and narrow is not an option. This journey is full of curves. Before he was diagnosed with anything I wanted to play safe. Let's *stay on the straight and narrow please.* Not anymore. Why be stuck on the straight and narrow when the curvy, bumpy, scary road holds something much more powerful and invigorating?

AJ is, by no means, static. This applies to the simple idea that he can only sit still for a very short period of time. This also applies to his ability to adapt and flourish wherever he ends up. He finds those signs that say "Road Closed" and busts right through them. I love his bravery and gusto. Everyone should live with that lack of fear and vigor for life, shouldn't they? *Of course.* And they should learn as much as they can along the way.

CHAPTER 14

Two Mothers

When I first read AJ's referral, I became taken with AJ's birthmother. She was beautiful, with eyes that spoke a million thoughts through just one picture. I studied her face, her eyes, her soul. We are the same age. *How beautiful, tangled, and broken is that thought?* The staggering truth is that I would not be a mother if it had not been for her courageous decision to give AJ a life of opportunity and the care he needed. She brings tears to my eyes even as I write this. She is so much a part of me. She knows where our son is, who Jeremy and I are, and I pray she knows my eternal gratitude and my love for her. If we would have met, I imagine it would have gone something like this...

Two Mothers

The road had changed from tired and worn to smooth fresh blacktop. We had passed blocks and blocks of crowded streets with utility poles littered with political flyers. As we drove further out of the city, the landscape changed as did the population. My mind wandered between our tour guide's continuous facts about Guatemala and the fact that I was in a third-world country just one day away of becoming a forever mother.

I had been so excited to see the Starbucks coffee fields on our way to Antigua; such ridiculous commercialism that is drilled into our brains. Perhaps I was using that excitement to mask the shear amount of fear I was feeling about meeting our son's birthmother. This trip to Antigua was not for the faint of heart. It was not simply for pleasure and tourism. It was to meet the woman who gave me the ultimate gift of motherhood.

Our guide shared a short, yet gruesome overview of Guatemala's civil war that had ended just a few years ago and still held ground in this corrupt country. He switched gears engrossing our thoughts with stories of active volcanoes and the idea of exploring them. We kindly declined and felt the road change once again. Oh it was a bad idea to wear sandals, I thought. The cobblestone roads were just as rustic and bumpy as they should have been. As we bounced around the van, my eyes began to take in the amazing architecture of Antigua. The surrounding landscape was bountiful with lush greens, volcanoes, and thick fog lining the very tops of the volcanos. The sun was shining and the breeze was adequate. I felt like I had stepped into postcard.

We toured the jade museum, carefully choosing jade pieces for our son's Godmothers. We toured countless churches and convents, marveling at ancient building practices and the beauty that lies within tradition. The streets were an even mix of tourists and natives, with the sweet-tempered music of the marimba playing softly around every corner. I gently squeezed Jeremy's hand in effort to transfer some of my nerves to him. My effort failed. We continued on to one of the oldest convents in the city. It was no longer in use, but yet I felt a calming presence as we walked in the old, heavy wood and iron doors. All of these places had nooks and crannies that served definite purposes. Exploring the history of a place in your own mind leaves room for a myriad of interpretations.

Imagery and purpose can be found in anything. We wound our way up a beaten stone staircase, revealing a magnificent fountain in a courtyard several levels below us. The water was still, but its presence was flowing. The fountain was created as a multi-pointed star with two levels. The sun gleamed off the water, giving its surface a transparent green tint. I smiled at my husband, realizing this was moment to breathe and take a moment to accept realization. Among all of this beauty, we were about to become parents. I realized, in that moment, what was truly beautiful and breathtaking in my life.

We moved on to the Cathedral de Santiago. This church, built in the 1500s, had been damaged by an earthquake and numerous civil wars. Constant destruction and construction had engulfed this sacred place. If ever there was a time capsule of Antigua's history, this was it. The church is deceiving to the outside eye. To really understand the beauty, you must step inside and walk through the entire building. As we walked through the ruins, I swore I would not forget a single detail our guide was sharing with us. We ran our fingers across the different bricks made of different materials, absorbing how many had tried to salvage the cathedral. Just before walking out into the ruins, the church opens up to the heavens. Quite literally. Arches of brick, with old foundations and new bridges revealed the picturesque white clouds and blue skies. Something so broken was offering such peace and perspective. Something worthy of greatness must withstand the test of time.

I suddenly realized I was comparing the Cathedral de Santiago with marriage. Marriage takes its own fair share of earthquakes and civil wars. Our marriage had been through much turmoil to reach the point of standing in that Cathedral and marveling at God's global presence. I stalled in leaving, knowing our next stop would be life-changing.

We had left Parque Central as one of our last stops in Antigua. Through our adoption attorney we had arranged to meet our son's birthmother. We had chosen Antigua as a neutral location, far from Guatemala city, far from the orphanage where our son was. I was nervously excited when I heard she wanted to meet with us. What would she think? What would she say? How would I understand her? How would she understand me? Is this right? Is this wrong? My mind played these questions over and over like a broken record.

Our son was born to this woman. She gave him his name. He was born at least a month early. I rejoiced the day we received his official referral packet. Oh how long I had waited to see that red and yellow DHL envelope in between the front doors. As I frantically flipped through the packet's contents, I stumbled upon more photos. A few I recognized from the initial referral email. But then, I saw these eyes.

A beautiful young woman, of Mayan descent, was holding our son in a photo with an orphanage worker. I thought nothing of it at first, until inquiring with our agency. Yes, indeed, the woman was AJ's birthmother. I sat in the rocking chair in our nursery for hours staring at pictures of her. As I began to read her profile, the tears began to flow. We were the same age. How had the stars aligned to join one mother making a choice collide with another mother making the choice of adoption? She had been raised several hours north of Guatemala City. She held a very basic education and worked as a housekeeper, as most women in Guatemala City did. I tucked the emotions that I felt while looking at the picture of her handing AJ over to the orphanage caged somewhere deep inside. I was too excited with having a referral and choosing baby names.

As we approached the fountain of fertility in the center of Parque Central, I saw her. She was sitting on a bench, facing the fountain. She sat prim and proper, rather unnatural and uneasy. I wondered if she could hear my heart beating from across the square. She looked up, locking her eyes with mine. She smiled a shy, quiet smile and stood up slowly. I stopped just short of the fountain and gently extended my arm to signal Jeremy to stop walking. She slowly stood up. We stood and admired, judged, surveyed, and pleaded with one another without exchanging a single word.

I waited for her to walk toward me. Eventually she did. She greeted me with a soft, sweet hello and slowly lowered her head. I returned the greeting and stood motionless. Jeremy and our guide had gingerly moved to a bench near the fountain in an attempt to give the two of us some alone time. I waited for her to speak the next words or make the next movement.

She guided me over to the fountain of fertility. We stood together and watched women walk up to the fountain, say prayers of thanks and prayers in hope of a having a child. This was sacred ground, and a sacred moment. I felt internally guilty about being an American woman standing in front of this beloved fountain. The woman was carved with great detail and boasted the essence of motherhood. Was I here to carry that essence on, or to cut it from her existence? I wasn't so sure.

As we stood there, the woman carved into the fountain became more and more beautiful. The water flowed freely from her breasts, filling the fountain below her and returning to her body to be used once again. She held her breasts tenderly, protecting that which gave her children nourishment and love. As the water sprinkled gently on our faces, tears began to roll down my face. She softly touched my forearm and looked up at me. Tears had stained her cheeks.

We slowly walked across the square and made our way towards the Arco de Santa Catalina. We chose an open air restaurant for lunch. Jeremy and our guide ate at a different table, once again giving us time together. How often does an adoptive mother meet and share the company of her child's birthmother? We both ate a small meal and enjoyed the afternoon rainfall. The cool mist after the rain was welcomed by the two of us, who were once again in tears. She grabbed my hand and squeezed it tight. We sat in silence, allowing our hearts to do the talking. I wished there was a way we could both mother to him. I had jokingly mentioned to my husband that we could cut him half in effort to share him with her. My heart was big enough, and from the moment I saw her, I knew hers was too.

Hundreds of questions flooded my mind as we stood there holding hands. So many things I could have asked her. Instead I chose to relish in the moment. I chose to allow our hearts to communicate instead of asking impersonal yet personal questions. After almost an hour, she let go of my hand and said we should go. I wanted to stay in that moment forever. I wanted her to know all of the things I had been telling her in my mind since we had gotten AJ's referral.

I stopped torturing myself over the lack of words being exchanged. Instead, I embraced the moment and enjoyed her presence and common interest. We walked to the convent on the east side of the city and stopped on the front steps. She said, "Gracias", squeezed my hand and walked to Jeremy, shaking his hand gently. She stopped on her way back to where she came from-ran to me-and hugged me tighter than I've ever been hugged. I hugged her back, repeating her parting greeting. Suddenly, she was gone. I sat down on the steps, paralyzed. Such a short period of time that I wished would have lasted an eternity. I felt trapped by emotion, lacking the strength to move forward in any way.

Our tour guide rapidly reminded us of our final stop on our Antigua tour-the public market. I brushed my heart off and we walked down the cobblestone street to the covered marketplace. On our way, I ran directly into a young woman who was carrying her baby in a sling on her back. My heart stopped instantly. She stared at me, I stared at her, and we went on our merry ways. I felt guilty the moment she left my presence. What were we thinking, taking a child out of his homeland? She stared into my eyes as if signal her awareness that I was a "rich-American" taking one of her own from her country. I tried to brush off this encounter with this young woman, but her face plagued my dreams for nights and nights after I ran into her.

We finally arrived at the marketplace and began to snake our way through each of the vendors. After being heckled and buying several pieces, we reached the quieter side of the marketplace. As I turned the corner, I saw a young mother in her twenties. She had one of the handmade baby slings around her chest and was selling her fabrics and handmade clothing. A little voice popped out from under the table and said, "¡Hola!". The woman's daughter had popped out in perfecting timing. A few moments later, I noticed the woman was breastfeeding her younger child in his sling.

The woman kept pursuing me and gently asking me to purchase some of her items. She even had a fellow vendor show me additional blankets and helped show me how to tie and the slings. This is not fair, I thought. This woman is younger than I am yet she must work with her children in tow. Life did not seem fair, not fair at all.

I fought tears as we climbed back in the van and headed back to Guatemala City. On our way back, our guide stopped in several different smaller cities and villages, most of them so poor it was heart-wrenching. In a small village outside of Antigua, I saw women sitting in a communal stone washing area, beating clothing on stone wash boards and doing laundry to make a meager wage. How is this possible? In a world of possibility, the people of Guatemala seem paralyzed by their own country and social system. This social system is what made AJ's birthmother unable to care for a special needs child and better herself.

I think of her often, wishing her peace and blessings. I speak to her aloud, often, hoping she can hear me. I pray she is not in pain over giving AJ a full life. There is a deep desire in my heart for her to know that he is doing well. I want her to know that we will never forget her; I will never forget her. Her beautiful eyes, her long jet black locks of hair, and the bright magenta shirt she wore the day she chose adoption for our son. The statement our son not only applies to Jeremy and I, but it also applies to she and I as well. AJ is truly a son to both of us. Sometimes, the spoken word is an unnecessary evil. We have a connection that can never be broken. I hope I am carrying enough love in my heart for both us. She gave me the gift of motherhood, and I embrace the role of motherhood as a gift.

Two hearts, two mothers.

CHAPTER 15

Buckle Up

AJ's 4th birthday was upon us and I was stressed planning his birthday party, as always. His birthdays are an honor and privilege for me to plan and celebrate and I was borderline obsessed with all the details. It is not about the stuff, it is about the privilege I have as his mother.

A few weeks earlier Jeremy had started feeling dizzy. His primary doctor thought it was labyrinthitis. We were told to go enjoy our long-anticipate mini-vacation to our favorite bed and breakfast over Memorial Day weekend. If it didn't subside, he'd see a neurologist the following week. We should have stayed home.

After cutting our trip short I took him to the emergency room as his dizziness was only getting worse. His symptoms also included tingling on his right side and on the left side of his mouth. They did a CT scan and sent him home with the diagnosis of dizziness and told him to follow-up with the neurologist the next day. We were entertained though...as the man on the other side of the curtain was handcuffed to his bed and was singing away and trying to schmooze the female staff. I will never forget that opportunity to laugh and breathe in such a scary moment.

The following day he saw the neurologist who sent him for an MRI of his brain and spine.

The MRI showed a lesion on Jeremy's brain. There he sat, on the phone with the neurologist telling me he had a lesion as I was walking out the door for my therapy session on how to handle my life with a special needs child. He said it so casually. "As long as it is not cancer, I'm good". *Well. I'm glad you're good buddy, because I'm not!*

Get ready, set, and go, for a mammoth race to see how many needles we can stick in your husband with and how many tests we can run. Initially, his incident was being considered a "clinically isolated syndrome." Meaning, a freak thing that just happened. The words Multiple Sclerosis (MS) started swirling around. We were given the option to treat with multiple sclerosis drugs, or not treat. "There is no definite test for multiple sclerosis" they said.

Wonderful.

It could be a freak one-time thing, or it could be the first flair up of MS.

Are we having fun yet?

Regardless if it is a one-time thing, the treatments could be preventative.

Mixed in all this fun was AJ's 2nd cochlear implant activation. I took AJ to school the day of activation, came home with lunch, shoveled food into everyone's mouths, and sped off to the hospital to have AJ's left implant activated. After the activation, Jeremy and I drove to his neurologist's office to hear the results of his spinal tap. "There is bad inflammation. Our suggestion is to treat. Here's 20lbs of literature to read. You will get better".

Jeremy didn't hear the "you will get better" part.

I did.

But it in that moment, hearing it didn't matter.

His symptoms were fluctuating, which meant his brain was healing. "A good thing" they said.

We drove home in rush hour in the rain. I gave him the good wife pep talk as we crawled on 43 South. When we stopped for gas, I sat in the car, paralyzed with fear, screaming and crying out as he was inside paying.

I wiped those tears before he got back in the car.

It was my job to be strong.

Strong.

We cried, we laughed.

Oh. "Happy Anniversary, honey".

We grabbed subs on the way home instead. If the IV steroids they were pumping into my husband's body weren't enough to kill the romance, his diagnosis was.

I pushed my husband around in wheelchair during AJ's last class fieldtrip at the zoo. Looks of pity made me want to punch someone and shrivel into a corner and bawl all at the same time. Encouragement from those we were with lightened the mood and helped us feel like warriors plowing through battle. He was at AJ's birthday party the next month. If you ask him, he doesn't remember being there.

We kept going. Even when we didn't want to, we kept going.

We moralize and minimize suffering.

It's all relative, right? —I find myself judgmental when I hear someone else moralizing another's suffering.

Well, at least it isn't as bad as Jackie's story.

Or Ken's life.

Or, hey, did you hear about so-and-so? Now that's tragic.

And the minimizing:

There is always someone else worse off than you are.

There are starving children in _____ (unfortunately, there is a choice of countries here).

The chemo's really not that bad.

So you lost your brother. It's not like you lost your wife or child.

Oh, you'll be fine.

Or my favorite....absolute SILENCE. *If I say nothing, it doesn't exist.*

I sat, mulling over these approaches to suffering, when suddenly, during a weekly talk, our pastor asked for a show of hands as to how many people have been diagnosed with a terminal or chronic illness.

My husband raised his hand.

MY HUSBAND.

Not the stranger two pews over. Not Nancy's third husband. Not so-and-so's father.

MY HUSBAND.

I placed my hand on his lap as he raised his hand. As he raised his hand, my tears began to fall.

And fall. And fall. And fall.

I am blessed, beyond belief, to have a stubborn husband.

Without his steadfast stubbornness to kick diabetes and MS in the rear, I think I'd have a wet towel schlepping around this house.

Jeremy does not schlep.

I sat, as my husband had a needle shoved in between his spine and awed at his ability to be logical and stay still with all the unknowns before us.

I turned my head to fight my tears.

I drove many miles in tears, praying to God that something would change and that this was not happening. I held his hand and gave him quiet assurance that we would handle whatever was to come.

I answered the doctor's questions when he could not. I watched him attend his son's birthday party, clearly in the clouds, realizing a year later that he wasn't able to remember the event.

I watched him go through two agonizing trials with different medications, both of which had more side effects than positive effects.

I watched his anxiousness before MRI appointments and slightly lose his balance on rough days.

I learned to read his symptoms without him speaking a word.

He downplayed everything to everyone else, but as the other half of this crazy partnership, I knew.

We are so incredibly lucky that his MS is slow-progressing.

His medication is working.

We take things one step at a time and pray.

A lot.

We pray in thanksgiving.

We pray in need.

We pray for certainty and guidance.

We pray for blessings.

But in that pew, I was faced with the raw (*and it was raw*) reality that my husband has multiple sclerosis.

And there is nothing I can do about it.

Me. The doer. The fixer of all things because I am the wife, mother, woman. *This.is.what.we.do.* As much as we are blessed and lucky that things are stable, it doesn't take away the bold reality that he has MS. We're a little spoiled by his success with the disease. It makes it easy to forget about the disease's possibilities. In that moment, I wanted to curl up next to him in our bed at home and lay for days. Just be. In all of this life's craziness, I wanted to just be.

I spent the next few days emotionally exhausted and thankful for the jarring reminder. I think I truly needed that. We are living proof that this is doable. *We are thriving in the midst of suffering.* We both give each other a learning curve and do our best to respect each other as we plod through this diagnosis. I try not to minimize when talking to others. I try really hard. I don't know how he feels, physically or how he feels completely on an emotional level. Men are hard to crack in that department. I do know that he has shown more strength and grace than anyone I've ever met. I love him more than I ever could have imagined when we met 19 years ago.

Sometimes we all need to be faced with that raw reality.

Sometimes I need to repeat it aloud.

My husband has multiple sclerosis.

We laugh.

I still cry. Sometimes.

As my father-in-law would say, sometimes *it sucks canal water.* But if there is one thing we learned from our experience with our son, is that you must learn to move forward when you can't change the situation.

Buckle up, sister. This rollercoaster just became a rodeo.

Buckle up sister. Here comes the raging' bull.

CHAPTER 16

Buckle Up...Again

That October morning began like any other morning with breakfast and the long ride to school. About half way there, I noticed AJ did not look right in the back seat. He looked dazed, like kids do when they first wake up in the morning. He was also blowing gigantic saliva bubbles and saliva was slowly dripping down the corner of his mouth.

I had to look back a few times to realize this was continuing...and rapidly pulled over. I jumped out of the car and opened his door, peeked at his eyes, which were pointed downward (again in that dazed eyes-half-open look). I ran back around the car and dialed the nurse's station at our pediatrician's office.

The nurse, who knows me by name, recommended I called 911. By the time I hung up with the 911 dispatcher AJ was fine...beating on his favorite vibrating turtle toy while smiling and giggling. I think I was hyperventilating, but I'm not exactly sure. A minute later, I heard the sirens and saw the police car come over the hill. I picked up a napkin to blow my nose and took three deep breaths. I was in no shape to talk much less share vital information. The officer opened AJ's door and took a peek at him, and then me, psycho crying mom.

Of course, AJ looked fine. He instructed me to stay in the car until the ambulance arrived.

Quickly I found myself outside, talking to one EMT while one other stood by for further instruction and the other started her workup on AJ. He was not pleased there was a stethoscope in his personal space. I shouted that the right coil of his implant was off and she promptly put it back on his head, as she had noticed them before I even said anything.

They took him, car seat and all, and strapped him onto the stretcher. I ran to the police car and told him I was leaving my car there...on the side of the road in the middle of nowhere. For some reason I had never noticed how far out we are until that morning..... I hopped in the ambulance and buckled in. They decided to go "lights and sirens" since AJ has a history of cerebral palsy.

This was AJ's first ambulance ride...and it was also mine. Somehow I answered all the pertinent questions correctly, in between trying to stifle my tears.

What the heck was wrong with me? Why am I crying in front of strangers? Weird.

They took AJ's blood sugar in the ambulance, which caused his finger to bleed the entire ride to the hospital. He was happy, except for the fact that the EMT was holding his finger to stop the bleeding. Thank goodness we took turtle with us....

I had conveniently parked about a mile before the freeway on ramp, so our ride into town was without complication. It was when we got off the freeway I **felt** what happens when drivers DON'T move out of the way. Ambulances lurch in this crazy way that I can't even describe...especially when they are going "lights and sirens" and at a relatively high speed on city streets. I asked the EMT's if that was annoying, and they responded that it happens more than you think. And I quote, "People are in a hurry...their morning Starbucks absolutely cannot wait."

I was jolted back into the reality that I was in a freakin' ambulance, with my kid. I was so worried about how he would do in the ambulance without me. He couldn't even see me. I will say though, he probably would have gotten a kick out of riding behind the ambulance...he loves lights.

We arrived at the hospital, where I learned one of the EMT's knew our house and knew Jeremy's grandparents. Small world. By the time we were at the hospital, my head was a bit clearer and I felt a bit at home. Home? Yes, home.

We were there for two hours. They decided to run labs and see if he had an electrolyte imbalance. We sat around for two hours, which AJ was really good for, up until the last 1/2 hour. Thank goodness I brought his backpack with his lunch in it. We resorted to playing with the water in the bathroom sink. He felt just fine, was playing all over the place and definitely wanted out of our little boxed in "look-at-me-glass-doors" room. The labs came back normal and we were discharged with "Possible Seizure", orders to follow-up with his neurologist for an EEG, and to give him plenty of fluids and rest.

My car was 30+ miles away. I wasn't really thinking about my car as I was reciting my son's birthdate to emergency responders. Here

I was with AJ, a car seat, a vibrating turtle, a stuffed moose named Tommy the EMTs gave AJ, and all of our belongings. AJ's fan club (*AKA the nurse's station*) waved goodbye as we were walking out. It was one of those days when I could not reach anyone to come and get us. A few hours later I reached a friend who came and picked us up and dropped us off at my car.

The next morning I thought I was going to have a heart attack the whole drive to AJ's school. I changed my route for a few days, and then avoided that road for a long time. I must have turned around every five seconds to check on him during that first drive post-seizure. I wiggled his foot each time I saw him stare off. Panicky, tired, over-stressed Mom syndrome.

He was fine. His teachers came out to offer hugs. I needed them, but didn't show it. It literally took me five minutes to pull away from the front of school after I dropped him off. Driving was not my favorite activity today. I stayed in town near his school, because the idea of driving back and forth again did NOT appeal to me. I did a grocery shop, talked with a friend, and went back to school to pick him up. He had a good day, much to my relief. I took a different route home, which alleviated some of the "driving past the spot where we got into an ambulance yesterday" stress, but I was still on eggshells checking on him in route.

He had his four-year-old check-up that afternoon...which of course, was clear across town. All in all, it was a good visit. Although I couldn't help but realize that we seem to have a pattern when visiting our pediatrician's office. The first time she ever saw AJ, we were in urgent care the day before....which was the day we brought him home. One of her questions was if anything had changed in our family situation...which meant I had to share Jeremy's diagnosis. I didn't want to share. Sharing meant thinking about it, which meant it would be on my mind for the rest of the day.

This is where I fold my cards; where I completely fold. No more hands please. I may be a super mom, I may be strong, maybe stronger than the average Jane, but seriously.

Even I have limits.

AJ seems to be just fine, Jeremy is doing well, but me?

Too much.

I fold.

AJ's EEG did reveal epilepsy. The abnormalities began almost immediately after the test began. Diagnosis number three. Of all the diagnoses he's received, this one hit me the hardest. Jeremy struggles with his cerebral palsy diagnosis, I struggle with his seizures. They leave me helpless. On the sidelines. Watching. Praying. Tears and fears abundant. Ready with the stopwatch and emergency medicine, just in case.

Buckle up, sister. Keep diggin' your heels in and stand your ground.

CHAPTER 17

Tender Moments

Being AJ's mother leaves me privy to many, many tender moments. Moments that continually shake me to my core and leave me on my knees in pure thanksgiving. These moments have the ability to stop the ways of the world and crush me into the reality of what truly is important. How precious life is. How precious this journey has been and continues to be. They remind me of the fragile blessing in front of me. They remind me of the tremendous fragility in our world.

He would have died.

He would have lost all function on his right side.

While listening to a seminar on attachment, I heard the diagnosis of Failure to Thrive explained much differently than I had originally interpreted it, way beyond the physical definition I had held it under for so long.

"...It is the freeze mechanism that is beginning to be understood as the Failure to Thrive mechanism. Just lie still. Preserve your resources so you can live for another day, another hour, another minute, but don't

hope anymore because you're going to die. Give up, lie back, death is inevitable. This short rather unscientific description of an infant's fight/flight/free scenario is not melodramatic. Babies do fear for their lives, in their simple yet complex understanding in reaction to not being cared for in the way that all babies deserve and need"-Dr. Lark Eshelman *Becoming a Family, Promoting Healthy Attachments with Your Adopted Child (Taylor Publ, edited ed 2006).*

Just lie still.

And wait.

Wait for the inevitable.

After reading this, I spent a few days shedding many tears, deep in the idea of loss. It made tremendous sense. His precious little body had changed so much from our first visit to his homecoming. His condition worsened and we didn't know why. He was giving up. My baby boy was giving up. How do I process this?

Sometimes the sheer magnitude of my son's life sucks the room of oxygen and leaves us paralyzed. I don't have an exact answer, science, or practice as to how to process his early life nor his everyday life today.

I came home from my women's bible study group and knew AJ would be awake. The sitter left and I gave AJ his soft tissue massage and put him to bed. A few minutes later, I heard him crying. The kind of crying that tears your Mommy heart out. The cry that comes with sad face, pouty lip, and no sound for at least a few seconds. It is very rare for AJ to be this upset.

I turned on the light in the bathroom, which is next to his room, and went in to comfort him. I sat down next to him and rubbed his back. He calmed enough to lie down and have the covers tucked on all sides of his little body. I snuggled next to him and rubbed his back. Suddenly, he cocked his head up to the side and was staring at the bathroom light through the air vent in the wall that is between the two rooms. A look of sheer terror came over his face and he started to panic and...cry. I quickly turned the light off and crawled back into his bed.

When we first met our little dude he was in a "bedroom" just off the baby play area in the orphanage. The room was very dim, with a very modern wood-blade fan turning slowly and the light on ultra-dim. There were bassinets lined up on all four walls.

My Mommy gut tells me that my little boy remembers. That he remembers lying in his bassinet for who knows how long waiting for someone to come and pick him up. I do my best not to think about his rough start at the orphanage, but his reaction to being in his room in darkness and seeing a soft light above him freaks him out. On another occasion we were laying on his floor with his body pillow and he looked out at the hall light-same face of sheer terror and panic. He scrambled into my lap and I rocked him. That was my first thought that he remembers.

From the very beginning I said no to the idea of putting a fan in his room. Don't get me wrong, the boy loves fans, but I could not put him in a situation that replicated his orphanage life. Something as insignificant as a fan triggered that desire in me. I fed him every bottle until he could hold the bottle on his own, because I knew he was bottle-propped. How long did he lay there and wait? While we often mention that he couldn't, see, hear, or use his eyes together before we brought him home, he did see. This boy's visual memory is incredible.

I continued rubbing his back while he fought his tiredness. He held my right hand while I rubbed his back with my left hand. He fell asleep holding my hand and breathing peacefully. I'm forever grateful that I am able to be there for my sweet boy. While he has bonded to us amazingly well, sometimes I just think he still needs to know we're here. There was a time where he would not allow us to comfort him, so I'm thankful for this tender moment with my little man. I'm thankful he's HERE. And I'm thankful that even if he can't say Mama, he knows who his Mama is and has found my purpose in his life.

Tonight, after Jeremy gave AJ a bath and he was snuggled in his bed, I went in his room to kiss him goodnight.

It was then that I recognized that stare. The seizure stare. I waited, and saw the drool. I dropped to the floor and watched my little boy stare into space and held his hand. This one was about a minute. A minute that felt like an eternity. I sat and cried silent tears while I watched my little boy seize. I watched him intensely waiting for my little boy to come back. And he did. With a big smile and a hug. Thank God.

Tonight is one of those nights that I feel so helpless. We do everything we can for AJ, but this is one area we simply cannot do anything for.

No mother should ever have to watch their child suffer. Watching my child seize is torture to me. Pure torture. I try my best to be strong for him and comfort him. Even if he's still, I want him to know I'm there. His seizure activity has been off and on recently. I really hope it goes off for a while.

I still don't understand why AJ's epilepsy is the hardest thing for me to handle. Of all the things he has going on I cannot get over the epilepsy. I worry about more brain damage. Sometimes, I even get scared that someday the seizures will be uncontrollable and will take him from us. Tomorrow, I will call his neurologist's office. To which the nurse will talk to me for a ridiculously long amount of time and talk me through everything epilepsy. It will probably lead to another visit, a blood draw, and maybe another EEG. All of which I hate. Perhaps it won't. She'll remind me that breakthrough seizures do happen. They are controlled most of the time, but sometimes one slips through. Was he drowsy? Yes. Then you know the most common time for seizures is drowsiness and during sleep. Yes, yes I know. Is he growing? Yes, like a weed. Well, then?.... I know, I know.

I'll be checking on him a lot tonight and am already anxious for his amazing morning smile.

The last of the leaves were scraped off the curb last week. A mix of rain and sleet seems to fall every few days. We've done entirely too much switching back and forth between sweatshirts and the whole winter get-up. Soups and hot cocoa have become regulars in our kitchen. I'm starting to think about putting up our Christmas tree. Some gifts are wrapped and hidden from peaking eyes. All these things-static. traditional. routine.

But among all this is one constantly changing little boy. He has amazed us in the last few months. There aren't enough words in the English vocabulary to describe how much incredible progress AJ had made. It has gently reminded me to enjoy each precious moment with him. Suddenly, his life feels like it's in fast forward. I am indeed not sad about this revelation. In fact, I'm delighted. Ask any special needs parent and I'm sure they'd agree.

When our children grow, in any way shape or form, it is monumental. How our children's lives begin is never far from our minds. AJ has recently designated himself as the official light-switch operator. It started with just his own light-switch in his room, but has since migrated throughout the house. Besides the obvious gains of cause and effect understanding, fine-motor, and gross-motor, the most important gain is the simplicity of the act. As I observed him giggling, turning lights on and off around the house, my mind was flipping like a view-master. From a limp, tiny child to a tall, ever-increasingly independent big six-year-old who is doing things we were told were very unlikely.

Keep flipping those light-switches kiddo. Change is a good thing.

There are streaks of pineapple juice on my wood floors. Dirty clothes are piled in the bathroom. I don't remember where I left his bath towel. There will be no mom-made lunch today and I doubt there will be dinner either. The lawn is out of control in the back and I just don't really care. The weeds in the front landscaping beds are up to my knees. There are four baskets of laundry to put away, but I don't care. A bag of recycling sits on the dog crate, but I don't care. I didn't brush my hair today. I didn't eat breakfast today.

I put on clothes and a bra when my gut kicked in and screamed we might be heading to the hospital today. I watched as my son vomited and seized while taking his morning medications. Time stands still when that happens. The entire world ceases to exist and I am his and his alone. I gave him a bath until the moment he seized in the bathtub. After his bath he attempted to walk around the house, which led to a seizure mid-walk, causing him to fall step backwards and fall into the wall behind him. Jeremy ushered him back into his bedroom and we placed ourselves on either end of his bed and watched him seize over and over. New seizures with a different attack method, different symptoms, different patterns. Different sucks.

I slipped into the bathroom to grab a roll of toilet paper, convinced my full tear ducts were a result of my continued efforts to kick a respiratory bug that was hanging on for dear life. Instead the next few hours held precious and grave moments with so many tears. I rolled the toilet paper around my hand and started a pile as I cried and cried and blew my nose in frustration, fear, and sadness. Jeremy and I talked about things we never thought we'd have to talk about; and we've had some awfully difficult conversations in our life together. The in-betweens of this conversation were filled with more seizures and both of us praying he would simply fall asleep and let his brain rest. Knowing AJ had missed all of his medicines this morning told us that was not going to happen. Still-we continued to pray. For comfort. For the seizures to stop. For some kind of solution even though our conversations were not revealing a clear answer to any of this.

We asked ourselves how long we could go on like this. We asked ourselves about the quality of his life. What good are we if we are exhausted all the time? We admitted the judgement we placed over people in the "old days" that placed their children in institutions. We understand some of the why now. *Some.* There is a reason he qualifies for state insurance as his care level is that which is typically provided at a nursing or hospital facility or institution. We asked ourselves what we could do better. What are we missing? Why does this have to be so hard? For HIM.

I was able to coax AJ into eating tortilla chips and juice and taking his afternoon medication before he made a beeline for his bed again. He began to cry so I sat down next to him. He grabbed my hand and let large alligator tears leak out of his eyes.

I know buddy. I'm here.

How on earth am I supposed to sit here on the sidelines and just watch?

I am his mother. I am his protector. I am his advocate. I am his comfort.

I am his comfort.

Whoa.

I am doing something. I am being his comfort.

A half-hour later my sweet boy was sleeping with his left hand holding mine. If I made any attempt to shift or move he startled and squeezed my hand.

Stay here mama. Please.

Although I certainly do not desire the events of today to reoccur tomorrow, much less ever again, I do wish that what I felt this afternoon would indeed linger. Everything stops. The air suspends all movement and I feel the world stop. It feels like something out of a movie with some incredible special effects. Absolutely nothing matters except my AJ. My brain has absolutely no recollection of my to-do list, those dirty floors, or anything else. I am laser-focused and ready for whatever he may require of me next.

Eventually movement begins again. The dust in the air moves slower. Everything seems more labored and still, less important.

Later I walked out the front door to those same weeds.

I still didn't care.

And I shouldn't care. I've made it a mission to bury the guilt associated with not keeping up. Things will have to wait while I'm being AJ's mom. I'm holding my son's hand while he fights the body he's been given. That is exactly where I am supposed to be. His simple request for my hand reminded me of what is important. It is not the car I drive, the clothes I wear, the purse on my shoulder, my brand of makeup, the stores I shop, my income, or the education I've achieved.

Please mama.

I'm here bud. I'm right here.

When he woke up it was clear he was feeling better. After dinner we ventured to a camp orientation for the camp he will attend this summer. Life always moves forward. When we walked into the lodge tears began to well up in my eyes. As we sat down at the table and answered questions the camp staff member was asking us, I felt shell-shocked I did not have to explain him or defend him. As we walked out into the campground I breathed a sigh of relief and thankfulness. It was perfect. I'm not sure I've ever said that in relation to any of AJ's experiences or programming.

His smile as we walked around the grounds was so precious.

He was still a bit weak but insisted on walking the path.

That's my boy.

He always rallies.

Always.

His journey shows me such sweet glimpses of redemption.

He makes me brave.

If you can rally, so can your mama.

CHAPTER 18

The Bar Stool

Core. Oh how almighty and important the core had become. I did not fully grasp the importance of this until AJ's PT told me the bar stool story.

"We are going to work on this because one day AJ will be in college. I want him to go to the bars, sit on a bar stool and drink a beer, just like his friends" –The Greatest PT Ever

The meaning of this story has evolved over the years. At first, it thrilled me that she said his name and the word college in the same sentence. I had heard "well, we just don't know" so many times, it was delightful to hear her confidence in his abilities, even when that ability was several years down the road. The bar stool taught me to look down the road, just far enough to see the light, but not so far as to see the dark. The importance of his core strength was blatantly obvious. He needed to gain a solid core for stability, balance, coordination, and strength. It wasn't about the idea of the bar itself, the beer, or the friends, it was in his ability to DO. Working on a skill in order to give your child the ability to do something is empowering. Every single parent feels this at some point. But learning what you can do to enable your child who has multiple special needs, that sometimes stumps the best of the best and leaves you speechless, is more than empowering. It is invigorating. It is life-changing.

As lack of communication began to emerge as his biggest challenge, the social aspect of this story kept me focused on the prize. He will have friends. He will socialize. He will communicate. I don't know how, but he will. He'll meet his friends after class and sit on a bar stool. Yes he will.

His physical therapist birthed that creed. He **will**. Because of her I never thought any different. She never hesitated in her treatment plan or in explaining what we were going to do. She saw his potential, even when I was waist deep in grief and gasping for air.

I didn't like her when I met her. She was straight-forward. Actually, more like blunt forward. I wanted to throw something at her as she walked out my door the very first time we met. She had just told me AJ was at the level of an infant. I questioned- no laughed- at her credibility in telling me such nonsense.

The second time she came to our home I fell in love. Yes, I do believe this is possible to come to a deep reverence for your child's therapists. When you spend years, yes I said years with someone, you get to know them well. In addition to knowing my son, she knew me. And didn't judge when I answered the door in my bright teal puffy robe on the one morning I forgot we had therapy. She knew when my heart wasn't ready for a big change and fed it to me in small increments. She delighted in seeing AJ and watching his progress. Not all therapists are created equal.

Almost five years later, she discharged AJ. I had come to the realization that he would have physical therapy forever. It just happened. We had just utilized physical therapy to reverse his functional scoliosis. I never saw a tangible end to his therapy. Not because I didn't want an end, but because it had become part of our lives. "You don't need me anymore", she said. Music and heartache to this mother's ears. I smile every single time I see a bar stool. And I relish the thought of my son sitting on one someday.

CHAPTER 19

Darkness

We didn't plan anything for AJ's birthday last week. Mainly because it has been nothing short of insanity around here. On a whim, I decided to take him for a birthday lunch at our favorite Latin-American restaurant. Since it was a beautiful day, I asked to be seated on the patio.

It was the most depressing lunch I've ever experienced. I went in with no expectations whatsoever, mind you. We take AJ out to eat enough that he understands the concept and since the boy loves to eat it is a win win. This was the first time I had taken him on my own, without Jeremy. His presence was sorely missed. Suddenly, I was whacked into reality land. My child doesn't talk.

In fact, he didn't make a peep the entire hour we were there. Our waitress was working way too hard to earn her tip and for some reason talked to AJ at a much louder decibel than she did to me. He didn't respond. "Here you go buddy," she said. He stared off at God knows what and continued to methodically dip his chips in salsa. "Are you hungry?" "Do you want a spoon?" "Be careful, it's hot," she said. Usually his lack of participation is deflected by the conversation between Jeremy and I and the server. Because we are talking, the spotlight is directed away from AJ's inability to talk. Don't misunderstand me, we certainly make him part of our conversations.

I asked him several times if his food was good. "Is it good? Mmmmmmmmm. Do you want your juice? Say, more please. Mommy loves you." I felt so foolish. I felt like I was talking to myself. A train passed and I tried my hardest to get him to look. *Its way too far for him to focus and see.* He ignored me. I picked at my enchiladas and did my Mommy duty scrapping the rice on AJ's plate into the middle to help him get it on the spoon instead of the patio. A couple was seated on the patio and I felt the eyes of curiosity shifting to our table frequently. Just ask what the things on his ears are, would you? I left a healthy tip (even though she annoyed me, AJ made a huge mess and I'm that person who tips heavily on behalf of my child) and we left.

I sat in the parking lot and bawled. Perhaps I shouldn't have picked his birthday to make such a journey solo. I really didn't think it was that big of a deal. I cried until we returned home, when soon it was time to change and schlep out to his first hippotherapy riding session. No time to dwell.

Lately, AJ's pool therapy sessions have been at times where the club's day campers are in the pool. Clearly, I am used to a quiet house because 25-30 kids in a pool make me cringe and go into sensory overload. But today, I could not stop staring at them. Watching how the children interact with each other and were just able to move their bodies in ways I can only hope AJ will learn to. How the lifeguard blew her whistle and all of the children stopped (ok, paused) and listened (listened like kids sort of listen). They were independent, as independent as grade-schoolers can be, and enjoying life. AJ was enjoying every second of his pool time, but I know the reality of why he's really in the pool. Today, I just couldn't turn reality off.

I've been hounded as to what we are doing for AJ's birthday, and to be honest, I'm sad about his birthday this year. I'm not in a mood to put on a pretend face and have a huge party, only to hide my true heartache at such events. I'm still debating on hosting a little shindig for his little friends, but I think that's all we'll do. Last year, I felt the need to press on with AJ's birthday despite Jer's brain issues. Considering Jeremy doesn't remember any of his son's birthday party and all AJ cared about was the swings, I'm not sure it was worth it.

I am not sad that AJ turned five. I am so proud of my little man. He's not a baby anymore and shows me more and more every day that he's turning into a little boy. I am sad that he does not understand the concept of "Happy Birthday" being sung to him. I am sad that he doesn't understand what a birthday is-even the childlike concept of *this is the day I get lots of presents and cake!* I am sad his hearing age is 7-8 months. I am sad his language age is 6-8 months. Months. Not years. I am sad at how many words and sentences I speak every day and I receive no response from him. At all. I am tired of hearing about all the things he has yet to do. I am sad he does not know his colors or numbers. I just read that most children at the age of 7 are reading chapter books. Say what? He can't sign or say Mommy when he needs me. I am all too often overwhelmed when he screeches or whines and I cannot decipher exactly what it is he wants. I melt at the sight of AJ's smile when he sees his little buddy at summer school and wish so very badly I could snap my fingers and provide siblings for him. So many things make me sad.

I remember sobbing, uncontrollably, to one of AJ's therapist's last year. It was the first time I've ever lost it (in front of anyone other than my husband) when talking about AJ. She had the balls to speak the truth to me and I stifled my crying until three years of holding it in broke me and I sobbed aloud, "It wasn't supposed to be like this!!!" She cried with me. I'm feeling that way again. Surrounded by the normalcy of others and our grave differences is literally suffocating me. Days have become unbelievably full of these hard moments. And I'm not sure why. I'm grieving. This is a fact. But why such a full-on sadness? I feel like we're stuck and things are never going to change or improve in regards to AJ's communication skills. Is it my fault? What I am I not doing enough of? I feel guilty for being tired and for getting angry that I'm doing all that I am supposed to and we're still not getting anywhere. Isn't this my job as a mother?

Hard Moments Are Hard.

Jeremy and I had mourned our infertility very differently. I moved forward from it before he did. My darkness fell when AJ arrived home. For those of you who think I'm superwoman, supermom, or super anything, I am not. I felt robbed of a happy ending. Isn't life like the movies, where you have the baby, or in our case bring home the baby, and life is wonderful?

We were thrust into special needs parenting from the moment AJ was put in my arms. I questioned myself for months after his initial diagnoses. I *knew* something wasn't right. Wasn't it my job to do something about it? But I couldn't. All that time I felt was wasted while he sat in Guatemala and I sat here. The phrase "If we had known" ran through my mind a thousand times a day. We could have been more prepared; I could have been more prepared. I could have researched, planned, and been ready.

But would I really have been ready? I don't think so.

I cried for days. I shut myself off from everyone. All I had to talk about was AJ's needs, AJ's care, AJ's issues, AJ's this, AJ's that. Eventually people stopped calling. "Uncomfortable" was the theme between our social relationships. It only made me shut myself off even more. I quit my hobbies and devoted every single moment to AJ. And it was not healthy. Yes, you read that right. I jumped head first into everything my son needed. I ate my stress. I did everything I could for him, while completely ignoring myself. I was depressed and constantly agitated. My husband couldn't do anything right. No one could do anything right. Everything everyone did was wrong and I hated the world. I didn't want to get up in the morning. I didn't want to go to bed at night. I resented my husband for his lack of involvement. I was angry with family and friends for not being directly by my side. I didn't care that they were uncomfortable. Imagine how I felt!

I was in a constant state of self-pity. As AJ's primary caregiver—it was HARD. Perhaps one of the hardest parts of this journey was the lack of relation to others, even within the special needs world. Who else has a child with the same specific major diagnoses? I have yet to find anyone.

You know that saying, it's all relative?

Nothing.

Nothing was relative.

The friend who complained with weak worry over her child not talking yet became my silent enemy. I would say nothing, or offer words of encouragement when really I wanted to scream. *"Do you know how lucky you are?! He'll be fine!"* The few playdates we had turned into a comparison battle in my head, where I would cry the entire ride home wondering why "this" happened to us. The world can be such a toxic environment that promotes anger, jealousy, comparison, envy, resentment, and competition. I mean it when I say toxic.

As we moved through the world of special needs I found myself in darkness in other ways. He's a cochlear implant user. He has access to sound and speech. Why isn't he forming speech?! He was potty trained and now suddenly he's not? Why aren't the Botox injections working? Why why why?

And it got harder.

Jeremy's diagnosis.

AJ's epilepsy diagnosis.

I did not understand why all of this was happening. When were we going to catch a break? The toxins were flowing as I fell on my knees in the cold, spikey rain and asked God "Why? Why? Why?!" My plea was exaggerated, elaborated, and ridiculous.

Don't tell me God only gives children to special people. Don't tell me he knew what he was doing. Don't tell me there is nothing that

God and I can't handle together because right now, I'm in it and I'm not handling it!

Bitterness was eating away my very being. It was ugly. My only momentary grace was being able to compartmentalize my struggles and continue to care for AJ.

After some rather forceful encouragement, I broke down and began seeing a therapist. Not once did I ever cry in her office. Not once. All of these experiences had filtered my emotions a bit. I was able to control my emotions and share my story, my feelings, and all my heartaches without blubbering through it.

Therapy was incredibly therapeutic, as it was the beginning of taking time for me. It was the first time I truly heard, "What happened to you was not normal. It was not right. You experienced trauma." Sure I had heard "What happened was not right!" a thousand times before and even listened to other people's anger on our behalf, but this was the first time it sunk into both my brain and my heart.

While I thought I needed an army, I needed a friend.

This was my chance to beginning focusing on me. The environment forced me to that place. I certainly was not making time for it outside that office. At the time I felt like our goal and plans were silly and unattainable.

I spent time learning how to balance my needs with the needs of my family. I had forgotten myself in so many ways I felt unrecognizable in the mirror. Who is this person? What happened to Heidi? Isn't this what I wanted? To be a mother? To hold that title and all the glory that comes with it?

I stopped blaming. My bitterness eased. I began share AJ's story and instead of declaring "we didn't know" at the end of my cadence I made room for pause. That was progress. I began to process emotions I had hidden in anger for years. Anger is such an easy way to waste life. I didn't want to be angry anymore. I wanted out of the dark hole. I didn't want to sound like a constant complainer. Life was hard—all the time. Bottling that up proved to be detrimental. I was focusing all of my energy in the wrong place. I was attempting to change the things I could not and ignore the wisdom to know and harness the difference between.

Reflecting on the darkness is not easy. It is not without pain and some gentle regret. Wasted energy and wasted effort. What I have learned is that no one other than me had the ability to move from the darkness. *No one other than me.* As hard as others tried to pull me from the abyss, I wasn't moving. I tried. Oh, did I try. But I was stuck. Stuck in what should have been, what should be, and everything that was wrong in between. Darkness is such a cruel misinterpretation of reality.

We weren't promised easy lives. Wherever did we conceive the notion life should be easy? In fact, this premise bothers me greatly. Nowhere on the path of life is there a sign that states Easy Road, Easy Street, or Easy World. I have looked under the boulders of despair and around the wicked waves of bitterness and anger. I choose to walk into the light.

Dear Mommy,

I really enjoyed our time together on Friday. I love it when you swing me higher..and higher... and higher. Can you tell? My smile and giggles are all for you, Mommy.

I'm sorry I made you cry almost all day long. I'm finding myself, Mommy. I really am. Isn't it cool?

I know you were crying tears of joy and pride, but I still hate to see my Mommy cry.

Yes, I carried that big blue ball across the yard with both my hands. Yes, I walked while carrying that big blue ball. I know you cried. It's ok Mommy, really.

Yes, I hung from the rings on the swing set and giggled when you thought I was holding myself up when in reality, my feet were on the ground. I am taller and stronger, Mommy. Isn't it cool?

Yes, I handed you my cup and my bowl when I wanted breakfast, and waited patiently for my waffles and eggs. I am learning patience Mommy.

When you said "Stop!" as I was running down the driveway... I stopped Mommy, I stopped. Are you proud of me?!

Mommy, I have friends! I have lots of friends. Isn't that cool?!

I've learned a lot of new signs, Mommy. Isn't that cool?! I love being able to communicate with you.

Have you noticed that I am less frustrated and less aggressive? I love it. And I know you love it, Mommy.

Mommy, thanks for the iPad. Best.gift.ever. I love having a way to tell you what I am thinking or feeling. Isn't that cool?

Thank you for swinging me every morning. My body feels so much better when I get to swing before school.

Did you see me turn and walk out the gate when I heard the sound of the gate opening? Isn't that cool?

I know you see me when you call my name and I stop when I hear you call me. I love that you call my name, Mommy. It makes me smile and giggle.

Mommy, have you noticed I'm Mr. Independent. Thank you for fostering that independence.

I love seeing your happy face every morning when you come in my room. Do you love seeing my face too, Mommy? I think you do. You tell me I'm the most handsome boy ever every. single.morning.

I'm full of surprises, Mommy. This is only the beginning. Are you ready?

Mommy, I love you. And I'm proud of me.

Love, AJ

CHAPTER 20

Light

I've written before about my sweet boy's amazing morning smile. I've been trying to capture a picture of his early morning cuteness and well, it shouldn't surprise you that he turns into Mr. Growly Face when he sees my phone in my hand.

It is usually mid-afternoon when my patience begins to run thin. The removal of his left coil has occurred 8,438 times. He's tired, I'm tired. We're a mess. We somehow make it to and through dinner. We move on to bath time, which always brings a huge grin and rapid signing of the word "bath". Bedtime follows, with the hugging of the greatest pillow ever and the tossing of his lavender-scented stuffed Labrador out of his bed.

Bedtime brings much needed rest to my little man and moments of peace for me. It is the only time of day when I am too tired to think. My mind shuts off, for the most part, and I do my best to stay awake until a non-ridiculously early time for bed. Some nights I sleep well, some nights not so well. I never know what the night will look like. Night-time is my time. Whether I'm out with the hubs at a movie, with a friend, doing homework, laying on the chaise with the laptop, or sleeping, it is my time.

When morning arrives, I open AJ's door and find this smiley, happy little boy. It's like Christmas every morning. And I sure do love my present. He is so excited to see me! If he could talk I'd imagine he'd say things like "Mommmmmmmmmmmy!" or I don't know, something else in a really excited voice. It is by far, my favorite part of the day. It rejuvenates my soul to start the day and get my little man up and at 'em. I forget about yesterday's lack of patience. I don't think about therapies, or splints, or spasticity, or communication modes, or calories. I think about nothing and enjoy my son's amazing smile.

We recently took a weekend trip to a cottage up north. A special moment occurred our last morning at the lake. We shared a room with AJ, which had a full bed and twin bed. We heard him get up and did the whole "pretend we're sleeping gig". That lasted all of one minute, when I had to pop up and peek at him. He saw me and crawled off his bed. I was sure he'd walk to the door. Instead, he wandered to the side of our bed and climbed up and over his Daddy. He cuddled with us for a few minutes. And it was amazing. This was the child who took years to warm up to just our bedroom, much less our bed. He has never cuddled, in bed. Ever. It was a sweet, sweet moment for both of us. Another gift we've been waiting a long time for.

So many mornings I woke up to an empty crib, filled with heartache. I am so blessed to see his amazing morning smile. Every day.

Yesterday was a day which usually lives only in dreams.

As he does every morning, AJ flashed me the biggest grin in the history of grins when I opened the door to his bedroom. This moment, each day, is by far my favorite moment of the day. I drove AJ to summer school enjoying the sunshine, the cool breeze, and my recent iTunes uploads. After dropping him off, I ran to the store to purchase Jeremy some new duds for work. I picked up a very happy boy from school and we came home for a snack. Back in the car we went, with AJ's smile in full force.

We drove to the post office, where AJ charmed the hearts of every single person in the building. Our next stop was the grocery store, where he proved he is officially too big for the child seat. He did well as I encouraged him to "hold on to the cart" as I was packing the groceries. We stopped at his favorite Chinese place for his favorite fried rice, and came home to eat lunch with Mr. Smiley.

He laid down for a nap while I packed more boxes and did homework.

After waking up from his nap, AJ was delighted to discover we were once again leaving. As we walked up the gravel road to the horse arena, his little eyes lit up like diamonds and he squealed in delight. "Horses! Horses!" I could feel him saying from his heart. AJ enjoyed every second of his session and had his own giggle-fest when the horse trotted. He left cool, calm, and collected.

When we arrived home, AJ fully cooperated in the second favorite part of my day. He saw his Dad, and erupted with a huge squeal of excitement as he ran toward his Daddy. It is the sweetest moment I get to witness between my two boys.

Days like this fill me with positivity, hope, and a taste of the normal. While technically the day was jammed with summer school and hippotherapy, which are both educational and therapy....for once, it didn't feel that way. I cannot express how refreshing it was.

Monday was our telephone hearing regarding our appeals for the denial of AJ's physical and speech therapy. In preparation for the hearing, I spoke with AJ's PT. She listed all of the things we manage for AJ, and said, "You need to ask them when you get time to be AJ's Mom." That sentence has been on my mind all week. This is perhaps, the very reason, why hard moments are the way they are. While I am AJ's Mom, I am all too often wearing multiple hats at the same time. The Mom hat seems to be less worn than those that are seasonal.

Yesterday was a day full of sweet moments; moments where I felt like just a Mom.

◦◦◦

Where *IS* the light?

It's in my boy's beautiful brown eyes.

It's in his fearless climbing and loves for swimming and water.

It's in his silly chips and salsa face grin.

It's in my husband's sarcasm and joking manner.

It's in the joy and teaching of humanity AJ brings to those around him.

It's in his ability to use sign, his iPad, and rapid-method prompting to communicate his wants, needs, and cognition.

It's in his amazing perseverance.

It's in his infectious giggle and megawatt smile.

It's in his independent walking and daily living skills.

It's in his ability to eat apples like you and I do and stab his food with a fork.

It's in his interactions with his friends and those who love him.

It's everywhere on this magnificent road we are traveling.

A fellow special needs mom once shared a powerful visual with me. She told me that we needed to keep going; eventually there was going to be a light at the end of the tunnel. For years I debunked her claim. We must have taken the forest-like path because I wasn't seeing light. I now know I wasn't looking in the right direction. I so deeply wanted the light to jump out and flash in front of me like a bolt of lightning. Isn't that how I want most things, front and center so I don't have to put forth the effort to see them? Light is everywhere. Even at the end of a dark tunnel or that dark road that curves around the corner. You just have to keep going.

I chase the light. I keep going even when it feels like I cannot. I dare to see the light. I dare to believe I can infuse myself with positivity. I am actively attempting to see the positive and embrace it, fighting the habit of negativity.

I am chasing the light.

CHAPTER 21

Rest Stops

Sometimes we live life in the fast lane and sometimes we are in the slow lane. Who am I kidding? Most of my life is in the fast lane feeling desperate for the slow lane.

Often I feel like I'm stuck in traffic. I'm stuck at a red light at the intersection of School Street, Therapy Avenue, and Physician Boulevard. The constant phone calls, emails, consults, and inquiries close me in as if I am sitting in rush hour and I'm running out of gas. On most days I am running out of gas. Other times I feel like a traffic controller. Standing in the middle of the intersection with my orange vest and whistle, I frantically wave my batons trying to direct everyone. I'm the link between every person on AJ's team. Sometimes I'm able to control the flow of traffic between certain parties. Other times it is completely out of my control-craving hands and I'm stranded in the middle pulling my hair out. There is literally no escape.

In those instances I want to run to my car and drive to the nearest rest stop. I love rest stops. I love the little sigh of relief they evoke when that blue sign is spotted on the highway. I love how timeless they are; beautiful and practical at the same time.

Sometimes rest stops reveal themselves in odd places. A few years ago I attended an event called Women of Faith. It was my first time attending, and I wasn't sure what to expect. A bunch of Christian, Jesus loving women in an arena?

Whoa.

I was just dipping my toe in the God water when I decided to attend this conference. I was seeing God, but I wasn't seeing God in my life specifically. But I still went. I listened to an amazing group of women speak. I listened to the amazing Amy Grant's voice soar over our miseries. While the entire experience as a whole was amazing, there was one particular speaker who suction-cupped my heart from the first word that came out of her mouth.

Her name was Brenda Warner.

Have you ever listened to a story and felt your stomach tie up in knots, just knowing the story is about to go south at any moment? I was feeling the knots. I was feeling all the feels.

Brenda shared her life story, which included raising her son— who is blind. My tears began when she shared that her son's well-baby check was the only appointment she didn't mind because that was normal. Every other mom was taking their child to that appointment. She shared her life story and how it changed dramatically time and time again. She shared how God had worked IN her life; a life that mirrored mine.

Gulp.

As she went on my chest became so tight, I lost it. I had such a visceral reaction to her raw honesty. I'm pretty sure I was beginning to hyperventilate while failing miserably at trying to hold myself together.

Yeah, you look like a bawling moron because you are just that.

Not that moron part, but the bawling part. My sweet friends offered hands and squeezes of comfort and love making me cry even harder.

This journey has been so hard, and it is rare for me to have, much less be forced into, a moment to meddle in its rawness.

I was so busy doing I hadn't given myself time to sit in the raw.

Sit in the raw and grieve.

Sit in the raw and be human.

Sit in the raw and understand the gravity of reality and how it had changed me.

Her son is now grown, lives on his own and is thriving. How do I know? She brought him out at the end of her story. She shared him with all of us. Most of all, his perspective on life was refreshing. He survived. He lived. He thrived. He had a future. She did it. Through all of the struggle, heartache, crappy phone calls, and her journey with trusting God, she did it.

At some point, I felt myself shaking and ran for the bathroom. After I did some forced deep breathing and tried to focus my attention on the poster attached to the stall door, I walked back through the concourse to my section. Two friends stopped me just outside and said, "You have to come and see this, her son is singing with Amy Grant. I stopped dead in my tracks. The voice of a modern Joni Mitchell and this amazing young man were too much. I stood with them for a few minutes on the platform to our section, choking back more tears and fighting that visceral feeling again.

I've thought of Brenda a lot since then. I treasure her personal delivery of her story during that women's conference more than she'll ever know.

Raising AJ has been a constant flight or fight choice. I've always chosen fight. Doing so numbs you a bit. You just do. And process your emotions later. Sometimes they creep in, like in the heat of the moment, but the flight kicks in and the emotions are tucked away again. Listening to Brenda's story forced me into a place I don't go. Really, I don't.

Sometimes I find it hard to relate to other mothers. Ok, a lot of times. Gone are the jealousy, bitterness, and anger toward them for their normal-or whatever I assumed their normal in general to be. Here was this complete stranger, hundreds of feet away from me and she's got a suction cup on my heart. I kept nodding and bawling, nodding and bawling. She got it. She got me. She got the struggle. She got the triumph. She got the joy. She got the humbleness. She got it all.

Today, I was sitting in the neurologist's office with AJ as the nurse was asking me the questions she asks me each time we are there.

I stopped dead in my tracks with her last question. Any other specialists? I had no answer. I ran through my mental Rolodex of "AJ Providers" and nothing came up. I said, "No. Just you."

One.

Suddenly, having a pediatrician and just the neurologist added to the mix made me feel like every other mom on the planet. I felt liberated and ecstatic for my little boy. Oh wait, there is another! The dentist. Oh wait! He's normal too!!! We are down to one. One extra. And you know what? One extra is just like that well-baby check visit. I didn't mind.

It is hard to turn my internal GPS off. The part of me that runs constantly on all cylinders to be the best I can for my son. Sometimes it needs to be plugged in a recharge. Sometimes it needs a shoulder to cry on. Brenda gave me her shoulder while on that stage. I didn't even realize I needed it.

CHAPTER 22

Repaving

Construction season is constant in Wisconsin. The groans begin in early spring when the orange barrels begin appearing and the quarterly city newsletters boast about the upcoming construction projects. Last summer our road was on the docket to be repaved. I immediately groaned upon seeing and hearing the enormously loud piece of machinery that was essentially scrapping up and grinding the old blacktop that was our road.

Every day I said unkind words to the small barricade that was too many inches on my driveway, causing me to back out of my driveway like a student driver. Each day I cringed at the sound of my car driving on grated concrete. The smell of the fresh asphalt sent my olfactory system into overdrive and disallowed me from smelling anything else for weeks.

Whenever we're in the middle of a project which requires loads of grace, I find myself blinded by the progress. The progress required to get from Point A of the project to Point B of the project often encourages my tired soul to throw in the towel. I just want to get there. Without the work. Without the effort. Without the progress.

I need a fresh coat of blacktop every now and then. I may even paint new yellow lines. I don't need to worry about them being straight. The road will change.

And by blacktop I mean copious amounts of grace.

Confession: I am terrible at giving myself grace.

For years I have struggled with giving myself grace when things have gone askew with AJ.

Sometimes the praise and encouragement I've received as a mother feels like I'm on pedestal. This pedestal does not feel sturdy to me whatsoever. It makes me feel as though I might fall at even given moment and screw up.

Royally screw up.

"You know your child better than anyone."

Whew. That's a little bit of weight. I will call this statement both true and false. I do know my child better than most, but I don't know everything about him. If something happens, even if it is completely out of my control, I feel responsible. I feel as though I could have or should have done something to prevent that something from happening.

Hello my name is Controlly McControllerson.

Somehow I created the fictional idea that if I failed him in any way I was not giving him the best life possible. That was my responsibility after all-to give him the best version of life that I could. While I never put the expectation on AJ to be perfect, I was subconsciously putting that expectation on myself as his mother. Instead, I now strap on my steel-toed work boots and repave myself with some much-needed grace.

In those moments I feel like cannot do this? Grace.

On those days when the weight is too much and I cannot do this? Grace.

In all of this. Grace.

Our culture boasts "you can do whatever you want to."

I am all for that but—we tend to deny and ignore natural limitations. We all have them.

When we chose cochlear implants for AJ we knew he wasn't going to be the model candidate and user. Little did I know he'd swing so far left. We chose the method of communication for him that we thought would be best for his circumstances. His fine motor skills paired with his cognitive delay would not allow for him to use complete sign language. Today he uses a handful of signs; all of which have a target. For example, the sign for "please" is tapping the middle of your chest with you hand. That has a target on his body. Any signs that are done in the open air our out of his wheel house. The sign for "bathroom" is creating the letter "t" by placing your index finger over your thumb and doing a stiff wave or shake with your arm in the air. That sign is not in his repertoire. I spent years feeling as though there was something I could do to allow AJ to be more successful with his cochlear implants. As he struggled to make progress I struggled with the constant questions from outsiders wondering why he wasn't making said progress.

He had all the tools.

I sought advice from people who did not know AJ in hopes that they'd tell me something I had magically missed somewhere along the way. We tried new therapies, methods, and rituals. I sat in therapy sessions with false hope that this was the way he would start doing all the things he wasn't doing with listening and speech.

A public admission: I wasted time.

I am a firm believer that when looking at the big picture, nothing is wasted. But in this case, I realize now that we could have spent that time doing something much better than chasing after something that was dangled in front of me with glitter and rainbows.

I took the bait.

What I did learn from that experience was that sometimes, things just don't get better.

Sometimes things don't get better.

Sometimes, AJ is just AJ.

Last year I sat in a room with AJ's neurologist listening to him tell me my son has little to no executive function and little to no impulse control. This means my son does not know the difference between right and wrong or understand consequences for his actions. This means that he is incapable of controlling his impulses. His brain is not normal. This we knew. But this explained the lack of sleep we had all been experiencing for over a year because his brain was overstimulated and could not calm down. This explained his lack of understanding that knocking a lamp off the table and having the lightbulb break did not register with him. All of the nights we stayed up questioning why he was doing these things were explained.

And yet, I still asked what we were doing wrong.

Grace, Heidi. Grace.

I do not have to have all the answers.

I repeat. I do not have to have all the answers.

When we're in the process, all we see, think, feel, hear, and taste is that process. It's never going to change. The road will be bumpy, barricaded, and cumbersome forever.

Last year was also a season of aversion for me. I could not stomach any phrase with the word "season" in it.

"In this season of my life."

"In this season of life."

"This season of life is really difficult."

"Maybe you're in a difficult season of life…."

The word was everywhere.

I wasn't able to grasp the idea that my life has had seasons or that I was in a specific season. Perhaps I've been avoiding this word or concept of seasons out of bitterness and frustration. Social media boasts article upon article as to how to cherish your children when they are little. They won't be like that forever. You will blink and they will be off to college and on their own. It makes me want to punch something. Hard.

This is not a reflection of my life.

I was convinced I had only two seasons in life: life before AJ and life after AJ. In comparison to many of those articles things in my life don't change like that. We are planning our retirement with AJ here with us in some way or another. Friends would repeat the phrase in relation to their own lives or in general conversation and I would cringe. I may have been smiling on the outside but on the inside I was cringing like nobody's business.

Until my friend Denise and I met for lunch one day. We have the best conversations about the hardest things and yet I always leave her presence feeling empowered. As I droned on and on about my angst with this word she stopped me and said, "But you do have seasons with AJ. They just look different."

Well.

It took a few days for me to immerse myself what she had said to me. She was right. I find myself constantly challenged to remember that it wasn't always as it is now. Gone are the days of baby bottles,

Pediasure, private therapies, hearing aids, and a little boy who had no idea how to walk much less bear his own weight. When you are in it, you don't always see the changes. Things that in the moment I swore I would never forget because they were so momentous-I have forgotten. There is an ebb and flow to every life.

I find myself so caught up in the day-to-day. I can be so focused on the hard work that must be done to achieve his goals that I forget to remember and recognize how far he has come. I'd like another spoonful of grace, please. I moan on and on and on about the hard work and how I want it to be easy. I just want the newly paved road without the work that goes into it. I choose to grumble over the process rather than look forward to the new road that will be done sooner than later.

CHAPTER 23

Cruise Control

I have a love/hate relationship with cruise control. I find my own foot in control (surprise surprise) on the gas pedal is much more comforting then setting my speed to a consistent speed. It never fails that Myrtle the Turtle will merge into my lane and force my foot to tap the brake. What is the point?

I have a love/hate relationship with cruise control in life as well. It makes me uneasy that sometimes it takes a specific event or situation to knock me on the back of the head and realize life is so very precious. It is my firm opinion that none of us should be on cruise control-ever. It shocks me that I slip into it all the time. Perhaps it shouldn't shock me as I am human.

Cruise control includes sitting on the couch in a vegetative state while zoning out in front of your long-list of DVR'ed shows. It is not the actual action of binge-watching or taking time to relax that bothers me. In fact, I'm not relaxing at all. When I am so overwhelmed with life or paralyzed by fear that I cannot function I switch into cruise-control. Surely there is a better answer for me than zoning out. Cruise control includes ignoring what seems mundane today only to focus or hope for tomorrow. So often I miss out on the everyday goodness in my life because I am already fixating on the future.

There is a nature center close to our home that we have come to enjoy over the last few years. The property boasts an actual nature center with several trails and has one particular trail that is easy for AJ to navigate. The trail is paved and has railings to help guide his path and is just the perfect distance with enough dips, turns, and twists so that it is not boring. This trail is the perfect distance for him to be able to walk around it safely and enjoy his favorite environment. Nature is absolutely AJ's favorite place to be. I've come to covet this nature center quite a bit as well. It seems to be the one place where I am fully capable of quieting my entire brain and able to hear my thoughts without anything interfering. My list of everythings is very long. Everything ceases and I immerse myself in the place where I see AJ enjoy himself the most. All is peaceful and calm. The trees are majestic and remind me that the world is so much bigger than our problems. The sun shines through and I breathe in the tranquility. I hear the echoes of AJ's laughter bouncing in the air and smile.

This is the way life should be. I want to take in more of those moments and erase my entire DVR and submerge myself in creation. I didn't grow up a nature girl, but suddenly that's the place I want to be. I don't want to be on cruise control sitting on my couch binge-watching shows because my life is so chaotic that I can't function. I want more than that. I want to take the bad in stride and find good in the most mundane, ordinary, and simple things.

When we got married I loved color. I vividly remember picking out very specific towels from Target for our registry. Those towels were almost every color of the rainbow. Every single room in our house was painted a different color. Everything had to be a certain way. Perhaps it was part of spreading my wings with having home and exploring my tastes. I have since learned that what is important to me has changed over time. Back then I wanted everything to be very specific. When we looked at buying a different house, the choices we had were never enough. Whatever we lived in was never enough. Everything had to be bigger and better. I was drawn to the builder who did the six-panel doors standard and we would want to upgrade everything else. We were trying to keep up with the Joneses before we were even next door to the Joneses.

When AJ came home, my internal compass changed. It points to what is really important. No longer was I on cruise control under the spell of what I should want and what the world says I need. Cabinets and countertops do not matter when your son's life is in the balance. I have an appreciation for the old rather than the new. I have an appreciation for what is stable; for that which is vibrant and rooted. My husband, my children, my family, my friendships and this whole entire world that is at our fingertips-this is where I ground myself.

I used to joke with Jeremy that we could live in a cardboard box and I would be happy. As we have considered different living arrangements as life has gone on I've noticed that I don't care about the little stuff. I don't care about the towels. Towels are meant for a purpose-to dry my body. My body doesn't care about thread count, the cotton, or the tightness of the stitch. A towel is a towel. A sheet is a sheet. A glass is a glass. My heart craves old homes with charm and character and stories that would pour out of the walls if they could talk. I would rather live in a tiny house and spend our time together than sinking money into materialism. I realize that is a strong statement. Watching AJ endure everything his tiny body has endured in his short yet long ten years smacks me in the face quite often. None of the stuff matters.

I cruised right through life during my early twenties. I didn't really know about orphans, the orphan crisis, or adoption. I was completely oblivious to all of it (I was busy with the towels). Now I can't look away. When your senses are submersed in this word of orphans and adoption it is virtually impossible to ignore them. There are things that are wrong with this world that I cannot be okay with or ignore. I cannot pretend I have not seen orphans. I cannot pretend I have not seen their living conditions. I cannot pretend that group care is acceptable. I cannot practice ignorance, because ignorance is not bliss. I cannot stay on cruise control and ignore this.

I cannot settle into cruise control when the special needs world is too demanding and I want to quit. I cannot stop advocating for AJ. I cannot.

My foot is on the gas.

CHAPTER 24

The Future

My Gram used to tell a story about one of my uncles.

He had expressed his desire to join the military, even though he was legally underage. He stopped talking to her, in traditional teenager temper-tantrum form, and would direct all of his questions to Gram through his siblings.

Gram's boss noticed she was distracted at work and asked what was bothering her. She shared the situation; to which her boss asked, in his oh-so-pragmatic-voice, "So what's the problem?" She began to hem and haw and "Well.....well...," herself out of actual giving an answer as to why she didn't want her son to go into the military.

After a long pause her boss asked, "Anne?"

"Yes?"

"Do you have a scissors in your drawer?"

"Yes." (she pulls it out).

"Good. USE IT. Cut those apron strings."

Later that night during dinner my uncle asks his brother, "Please ask Mom to pass the peas."

She passes the peas and says, "Please tell your brother I signed his service papers today."

It wasn't until I was eye to eye with a 4-pack of fruit cups that I realized I too have apron strings. I know it sounds strange. Fruit cups? Most of the time the messes AJ creates at mealtimes don't bother me. There are few foods that bring out my sensory issues: oatmeal, the residue from cinnamon cereals, and fruit in syrup. Blech. Somehow, I started draining the canned fruit AJ eats before cutting it into pieces (when needed). I've avoided buying the fruit cups for a long time for fear of the syrup. And forget putting them into AJ's school lunches. Oh no, we can't have that.

These little suckers seemed to be haunting me. I debated and debated. And then I bought them. After owning up to my tight-tight apron strings. The only way he's going to learn is by exposure. Believe me, I've already applied this theory to many other situations that my brain debates constantly.

It isn't about the fruit cups, ya know. While I consider myself as AJ's advocate, even I have faults and apron strings. It has been a few weeks and I'm happy to report that AJ is doing just fine with his fruit cups a la syrup. He's also showed us that he is able to climb in and out of his car seat, safely, all by himself.

A few weeks ago I had the opportunity to join Jeremy on a weekend trip a few hours from our home. I initially decided not to go, for fear AJ would not do well with us being gone again after his rough reaction to our Hawaii trip. I decided to go. In addition, I did not write my in-laws binder of instructions. I gave them the basics (which they are already familiar with) for morning and evening routines and then wrote the words "HAVE FUN!" in the middle section of the single page of directions. I think that deserves some sort of control freak brownie points or something. I enjoyed the weekend and AJ had a blast with his grandparents. Another string snipped. He's growing up so fast. And I'm doing my best to let him.

The "f" word in my life is AJ's future. It's not something I talk about a lot. Looking that far ahead unsettles me. The more I keep trying to envision what his future might be like, the more anxious and depressed I get. For the most part, I've set my sights on the present of AJ and what he is doing, rather than what he might do someday. It's been a healthy thing for both of us.

I don't have my head buried in the sand. We have already determined guardians for AJ and continue to work on other logistics of his future. The thought of AJ in a home for the disabled? It makes me cry. My mind goes to bad places when I think of it.

AJ in need of a special home?

AJ without me and Jeremy?

How could we do that to him?

Who would protect him and take care of him like we do?

No, he could never go to a home.

But what if it were the right thing for him? He'll need to be somewhat independent.

Would he be able to change his clothes himself or would there be someone to help him?

GULP. How will he communicate his wants and needs?

What kind of friends would he have?

What do those homes look like on the inside, anyway?

What kind of job would he get?

How could I not kiss him every day?

How often would we visit?

And so on and so on. My mind spirals off into all sorts of irrational thoughts. And I know they are mostly irrational, given the fact that AJ is four-years-old and still has lots of growing to do and progress to achieve.

There is a home for adults with disabilities near a store I frequent while AJ is in school. A group of residents would come in sometimes; a mix of adults with mental disabilities. I'd spy on them the entire time as I'd walk the aisles, watching them talk, laugh and enjoy themselves, while shopping with the help of their aide. I felt glad for them.

On a different day I was at the same store; so were the group of residents. As they were checking out, I literally hid in the back of the store. Bawling. Thinking about AJ's future; picturing AJ as one of them.

The truth is, I'm not yet at the special-parent developmental stage where I can think of this. It's still too painful. And yet, what's helped me help AJ is researching things that could benefit him. While we celebrate each and every one of AJ's small successes and moments, the fear of the future is never far away. My child cannot communicate effectively to anyone what he needs or wants. THAT is scary. I wonder whether or not he'll be in college. I wonder if he'll have a job. I continuously wonder.

The constant back and forth is what drives this fear of the future. I have digested and accepted that my son is deaf and has cerebral palsy. It has been years since that was introduced to my brain. But AJ's recipe for life? It's FULL of ingredients. These ingredients seemed to be optional (even non-existent) in the beginning. He has this, oh now this, and well, this. Adjust. Readjust. Adjust again. Repeat. All of it makes me want to get off the merry-go-round and puke every now and again. It never seems to stop. All of these ingredients make constant changes to his future.

And for someone to say, "Oh, he'll be fine." You don't know that. No one knows that. Fine is not, and never will be a word in my vocabulary.

AJ deserves more than FINE.

I want him to have an extraordinary future, not just a "fine" one.

Fall is the time of year that makes me reflect. The trees are turning and the leaves are beginning to fall. My street is full of a unique blend of green grass, mixed with golden yellow and burnt orange sprinkles of leaves. Fall makes me feel like life is in fast-forward.

There used to be a home that was used as a CBR (Community Based Residential Facility) across the street from us which accommodated a few adults with disabilities. It was Halloween last year when I noticed something particular. While handing out candy to all of the adorable princesses and superheroes, I noticed a Christmas tree in the front window of this house. The tree was fully lit with those big beautiful colored glass bulbs that you just can't find anymore. If you do find them, the colors just aren't the same as the old ones. Jeremy was familiar with CBRs, but I was not.

Discovering the CBR bothered me for weeks. Ok, let's be honest. It bothered me for months. I had same pent up feelings as when I was in a local store and saw a group of disabled adults shopping in group. The future scared me and I ran from it. I didn't want to look at the house, nor did I want to pay attention to the coming and goings of the people that live there.

Shut it out. Tune it out. Make it disappear.

Thinking about your special needs child's future is a Catch 22. You have a hard time living in the moment because you know all of the things your child needs to do/accomplish/learn in his life. In the same breath, you don't want to think about the future because it is painful. Extremely painful.

I didn't want to think about my son being in a CBR. I didn't want him to be different.

Yesterday, my friend from the CBR did his daily morning walk and greeted AJ and I as we made our way to the car. I was sad when they took the Christmas tree down...even though it was well beyond the holiday season. I started to yearn for AJ to have the opportunity to live within the community...semi-independently. If you are thinking it is too early to be thinking about this-trust me-it is not.

My thoughts have changed and my heart has healed a little bit more. At this point, AJ would not be able to live in a CBR. Coming to that conclusion was painful. But once it was made, a little more healing took place.

Yesterday morning I looked out the window and saw the leaves falling and the breeze blowing the beautiful maple tree that stands in the CBR's front yard. The presence of the CBR is my constant encouragement. While AJ is my first encouragement, the house was my second. It only took a few weeks for us to realize the residents of the CBR had only moved just a few blocks down from us. There are new people in the house now, but that doesn't change that house from serving as a symbol of encouragement for me.

The future is a tricky bugger. If you had told me I would marry my high school sweetheart and lived the last twenty some chapters I would have laughed hysterically. My first year of college was spent immersed in an elementary education degree program. A blue binder filled with sweet pictures colored by kindergarteners (from my first clinical placement) still sits in my memory bin. I remember every moment with those kids and the experiences that field teacher gave me. A few years later I earned that associate degree which taught me medical billing, coding, transcription, and medical terminology. I had no idea what I was going to do with it-but all of those hours spent learning about those things helped me to advocate for AJ needs. That degree helped me understand the medical terms doctors spit out at us in so many appointments. I spent seven precious years taking care of my sweet Gram. Most of those years included taking AJ with me to her home or wherever she needed me. I had no idea at the time that caring for her would teach me patience, empathy, and prepare me for a lifetime of caring for AJ. Eight years ago I started a blog and began writing our story. Two years ago I earned my bachelor degree in English. Clearly those two things are related.

I had no idea how all of those things would play into my life. I haven't used any of these skills or degrees in the ways I thought I would have. I am not a teacher, a medical receptionist, or an English professor. What I am is a mom with a variety of experiences who is using those experiences to the best of her ability in a variety of ways. Nothing is wasted.

The outlook of AJ's future has changed many times over in nine years. I have no doubt it will continue to do so. Some days his future is full of inspiration and hope, other days it isn't an immediate thought because we are consumed with the here and now. Some days we operate minute to minute. AJ is the king of curve balls and the master of comebacks.

As AJ grows older his future often looks lonely. I hate that sentence. The thought often consumes me. As he has gotten older the divide between AJ and his peers has widened. It brings me great sadness and it a difficult reality to swallow. There are various factors that contribute to this reality, many that I strive relentlessly to change and improve for him. Yet, you can lead a horse to water but you can't make him drink. AJ shows no desire to be around his peers. I'm still trying to digest that.

I've also learned that we don't need the perfect place to "fit" anymore. I am not a fan of statistics, but imagine the odds of finding other parents that have AJ's exact challenges to be one in a bazillion. The special needs world can often be quite lonely. For me. For Jeremy. For many special needs parents. At times my struggles as a special needs parent parallel Jeremy's struggles. Other times, they are completely different.

Do not pity us. We do not seek pity, rather understanding. Understand that this journey is hard, completely worth it, and different. Understand that my son's disabilities don't make him any less of a human. Understand that I am not a saint, going straight to heaven, or in good with the Big Man Upstairs simply because I am a special needs parent.

We are now beginning to explore AJ's future. We are beginning to talk about middle school transition. What will he need when he's 25? What can we do now and throughout these next educational years to prepare him for where we see him at age 25? Sometimes it gives me hives. Will he live with us? If not, where will he live? What will he need? In the immediate, I wonder if he'll like camp this summer and how many times we'll go to the pool. Will his seizures continue to be controlled with medication? What is going on with his brain today? It is a delicate balance to stay in the present and not look too far into the future. I have hope. Hope that someday AJ will be wrestling on the floor with his own sibling or friends with target speech and enjoying life to the fullest. Hope that there will come a day where we are not swamped with paperwork or have to think about his disabilities with such intensity. If anything about his future is certain, it is that it will be full of hope.

Most of the questions I ask are answered with the scariest answer I battle with every single day: I don't know. *I don't know.* Occasionally, I am content in not knowing. Mostly, I am anxious, waging war with my desire and non-ability to control the outlook of my son's future.

I suppose that may not be the worst thing, though. It is HIS future.

CHAPTER 25

Souvenirs

Molly and I met through an online group for Latin American Adoptive parents in our state. I no longer recall the details as to how we ended up figuring out that we were using the same adoption agencies, but we indeed figured it out. We met one day for lunch, which sparked the beginning of a beautiful friendship.

Our friendship was woven with such a unique fabric. Neither of us had children (yet). We were both adopting from the same country, using the same agencies, and our children were in the same orphanage. Much later we'd learn that our boys were not only in the same orphanage, but the same room, just a few bassinets from one another.

Mol is a breath of fresh air. She's a straight shooter and doesn't mince words. She wouldn't be herself is she carried on with small talk and fluff. She has a deep root in sarcasm that is laced with the perfect amount of humor. So much humor and inappropriate laughter was had while we were waiting for our boys. Mol was the one person who was incredibly tangible in my life and was experiencing the same thing I was.

It still astonishes me that we picked up our boys at the exact same time.

She was the friend who watched my son when I attended my father's funeral. No questions asked. She was the friend who said "this sucks and I'm sorry" when that's really what I needed to hear. Mol is the friend who offers love, encouragement, and apologies all when they should be given. She is the friend who will call me out of the blue and we pick up right where we left off the last time we chatted. She always makes me laugh and leaves me in a deep wake of honesty that is blissfully refreshing. Our conversations always help me find the good in my life. Basically she's my hero.

Along this journey I have collected and treasured many souvenirs.

By souvenirs I mean friendships. Mol is one such souvenir.

She came in the form of a friendship I didn't see coming.

Mol always asks me, "So tell me what's going on. I want to know."

She wants to know.

Here's the kicker: Not everyone wants to know.

If there is one thing I've learned in my thirty plus years it is that friendships take work. They also evolve. There is an incredible amount of give and take needed from both sides. Other components are required, such as understanding, grace, love, and the tricky one: effort.

We have gained and lost many friendships throughout this journey. It is one of the most interesting and devastating things I've ever endured. While our world was changing, we craved normalcy. We craved our friendships. Our family dynamic is intense. *I get it.* That intensity is too much for some to deal with. For some it is too much to even talk about it. I spent many years feeling alone and isolated, marinating in that. Lost friendships added to that. The further south we detoured, the less people I felt near.

Let's be honest.

Sometimes we just need each other.

I had to pick myself up and find my people. Turns out I had to exercise some effort too.

A few years ago Jeremy and I were at a point where we were downright desperate to find support. We had heard whispers of a special needs support group starting up at our church and were beyond excited. Something happens to the Type A, organization freak, control freak in me when I get excited. All of those qualities become amplified and start chomping at the bit to come out and do their thing. Certain situations do not always require these qualities, nor do they always require these qualities specifically from me. Still, we went to the first meeting of this special needs group.

From that group we have gained several friendships that far surpassed anything I was thinking during that first meeting. Friendships that consist of late night phone conversations, texts, date nights, and holding each other upright when necessary. We do life in a familiar and relatable way. We may not drive the same car but we are in the same lane. We do a ridiculous amount of laughing and sharing knowledge. We speak in acronyms and IEP language. We practice kindness and encouragement. Because we have one another, the tears are less.

Somewhere along the way a friend told me we would have a rollercoaster of good and bad years. Specifically, she meant our relationships with AJ's school staff and therapy staff would offer both good and bad experiences. She was so incredibly right. Over the years we have had many, many, many people on AJ's team. I don't like to call these people staff members. That sounds too cold and distant for the amount of time these experienced humans have spent with my son.

These people have been his teachers, his therapists, his advocates, his planners, his encouragers-his dream team. I learned early on to weed out the ones who did not understand AJ. Those who made the cut have become not only his cheerleaders, but ours. These people have seen me in my bathrobe. They have seen me being mama-bear many times and have seen me at my most vulnerable.

I have lots of souvenirs from this journey. Instead of representing different states or countries, mine resemble the roadmap of my life. Some are from earlier in my life. Some are from college. Some are acquaintances. Some are from our life before AJ. Some are from a book launch team that became my tribe.

I have met the most incredible people being AJ's mother. Mol, and many others would not have come into my life without that opportunity. I have become friends with therapists, teachers, assistants, sitters, providers, fellow parents, and I am so incredibly thankful for my people.

People are way better than a coconut monkey or a keychain with your name on it.

CHAPTER 26

GPS

How do you do it?

This question is often asked when my counterpart to a conversation isn't sure what else to say. It usually comes after what I call the "Oh Factor". I coined this phrase a few years ago when the same simple and shocked phrase kept pouring out of people's mouths.

Me: He was adopted from Guatemala.

Them: OH! (with underlying tones of "How wonderful!" "How amazing!" "That's awesome!")

Me: He has cerebral palsy, blah blah blah blah. Them: Ohhhh. (Quieter, respectful, surprised tone with a pinch of "Wow you are a saint! God bless you!!")

Me: We didn't know.

Them: OHHHHH. (Slower, somber, slight tinge of insert foot in mouth, with nothing else brilliant to follow)

And this is where the "How do you do it?!" question comes into play.

I do not have a straight forward, knock-you-down-amazing comeback or answer.

I just do.

Something instinctual awoke in me when AJ was placed in my arms forever. I had this gut feeling that something was really wrong. Wrong? Perhaps that isn't the best way to word it, but my novice Momma instincts went with that word. Something was going on? Something was awry? Our road was going to be bumpy. Very bumpy. With dips, detours, traffic jams, and low visibility at many, many points. My internal GPS recalculates way more than you want to know.

Every single day I wake up to my son. Most mornings he greets me with that morning smile. Anything in my headspace clears immediately upon seeing him smile at me like that. Other mornings I may be greeted with cries of pain, fear, or he may be mid-seizure. All of those moments are just as beautiful as that smile. Why? Because he is HERE. I have many moments, even now, years after his homecoming, where I find myself with the desire to pinch my own skin and make sure this is all real. That my baby boy is here. He is alive. He is thriving. Because I know all too well that this reality may have only been a dream had his adoption case been delayed.

Sometimes it is NOT fair. Yes, still. Sometimes I scream. Sometimes I pray so hard my hands turn different shades of red. Sometimes I am so tired I do not want to get out of bed. But I do. Sometimes I am so happy and elated I cry tears of joy. Because that smile, and the boy behind that smile is just next door. And that blessing is too great to pass by and not partake in.

People told me to grow up.

Snap out of it.

It'll get better.

You're a saint.

I could never do what you do.

I was a constant sounding board for one-liners. None of them did any good. I needed to process my new role as a mother in my own time. I needed to process being a special needs mother in my own time. I needed to process all of it on my own time. There were times where I would find myself with the desire to shake my own shoulders and say, "Snap out of it!" It just wouldn't happen. Forcing the issue only made it worse.

Here's the thing:

There is no crown, no cape, no pedestal, no angel dust. Just a mom doing her very best.

While packing for a move a few years ago, I stumbled upon a book from my freshman year in college. Plato's *The Republic* was a game changer for me. I have no idea how my brain comprehended the contents. Seriously. I saved the book because it was used my in favorite college course, Foundations of Education, and reminds me of my favorite professor. Also, all my notes on the inside and back covers make me feel smart.

The first page I turned to shared this note I had written in the margin:

"No one should display bad character in anything that they do."

Am I displaying poor or bad character as a special needs mom? Am I setting a bad example?

The title SuperMom was given without my consent. I do not remember signing a release allowing that title to be used in reference to me, myself, and I. I was not given a costume when AJ was placed in my arms. No sequins, leather, or push-up anything. No costume, no super powers. My costume usually consists of undone hair, whatever clothes are clean (and most likely have some issue or another), flip flops, or tennis shoes.

And yet I feel like I have a responsibility to fill that role, without even thinking about it. I've devoted much of my blog to the ultimate truth about life with a multiple special needs child. Most of my posts have been borderline depressing. I can't change the truth.

So the question remains: am I displaying bad character?

Should I be putting on the smiley face for all?

A friend called me stoic the other day. I was shocked. Not an adjective I would have matched with myself. I cry. I BAWL. I lose it. I cry so hard I can't breathe. I get emotional. It happens when I least expect it. I equate it to being punched in the face a hundred times. Eventually, you get knocked out and fall to the ground. Sometimes, I'm so numb I can't breathe, much less cry. The crying comes a few minutes or hours later. People are programmed to respond to positivity. I've learned to spin some sort of positivity to spare the person the awkwardness and to spare me wanting to rip them to shreds for not understanding. It's almost as if "AJ's doing so great!" is supposed to erase all the difficulties we are in the midst of right now. It doesn't. As much as I truly wish it did, it doesn't.

So. Bad character?

Nah. Maybe I'm just a bad Mama-Jama who speaks the truth.

cape

Logistically, my GPS is constantly recalculating. When AJ was younger recalculating sounded something like this:

...I know we don't like the Theratubing around his leg idea, but it's only temporary until he gets his AFOs.

...I know he does well with the spoon and it is less of a mess when we feed him, but he needs to practice eating with a fork and eat on his own more.

...Did you see the new list of activities to help him communicate? It worries me.

cape

...Did I pick up the photos for his experience books? I have to get those up and running ASAP.

...Uh-Oh why is AJ taking two steps and falling? Uh-oh, his muscles are tight again. Is he growing? Does this mean he needs Botox? Will he continue to be tight?

...We have to get more Pediasure. I think I have more coupons, let's pray it is on sale. Did I hear if insurance is going to cover it yet? Reminder to call the insurance company.

...Sigh. He's freakin' hungry and he's mad. Where is our food? Why didn't I bring the fruit loops to tie him over?! If you get up with him he won't settle back down at the table.

...The insurance company is saying continued OT and PT is maintenance...yes, I already talked to his therapists about it. We need to draft a letter and fight this.

...We both need to stop carrying him so much and take time out of each day to help him work on self-care skills.

...When is the right time to potty train AJ? We said we'd wait till he started school and adjusted. Yep, we'll have to talk about that sooner than later.

...It's not good for AJ to close himself in his room and self-stim. It is not good for AJ to walk around with a metal bowl and not play with other toys. Let's find something else for him to do.

...How did AJ do in school today? We need to discuss X,Y, and Z.

My GPS recalculates all the time. Sometimes it is full of uncertainty, worry, problem-solving, discernment, and action. There is always something new to route and perhaps, reroute. Other times it is spot on and knows what needs to be done.

A conversation that took place with my friend Carrie runs through my GPS every day. I met Carrie a few years ago through our special needs support group. We had met a few times over the course of a few months when Carrie called and asked to meet me for coffee. She told me she had some things to tell me. Carrie told me she had read my entire blog in one night and thanked me for my transparency. It was exactly what she needed and was refreshing to read such honesty. In that moment, I knew I was meant to write about our journey. Her words stay close to my heart and always serve as an encouragement when I am unsure. I aim for that transparency, because if we aren't real we are the alternative. I don't want to be the alternative.

CHAPTER 27

Five Years to Healing

For a very, very long time I was unable to recall or share the good memories of my family's journey and my own personal journey. The circumstances, wrong-doing, etc. that occurred when we adopted AJ deeply overshadowed some very sweet memories. Everything in relation to our adoption became negative. Everything was wrong. I couldn't talk about the adoption without including all the things that were wrong. I couldn't talk about AJ's disabilities without being bitter. I was a sad, sad person.

Yet at the center of it, was this precious little boy; this human soul who was in the midst of all this pain and anger. I've always been able to compartmentalize what happened with the adoption along with my love and caring for AJ. Without a doubt, he is a blessing. But it was still an unfair perspective, to both of us.

It took five solid years, almost to the day, for me to heal those wounds.

Jeremy and I had cautiously and slowly brought ourselves back to our Christian faith. We had both been raised in the church. He was raised in the most liberal of the Lutheran synods, while I was raised in the middle synod. While we were dating we attended the church Jeremy grew up in and eventually married there. After we were married, we spread our wings with the idea that we didn't have to go to church now—so we didn't. When we received AJ's diagnoses, Jeremy and I both spent a lot of time being angry with God, putting the blame where we thought it should go. Bitter. Angry. Repeat.

The first Sunday we took AJ to church he let out a squeal that was rather loud. The entire church turned around and stared at us. We slinked ourselves back a few rows into the cry room. We were already convinced he had some level of hearing loss, so we were already on edge about "controlling our child" in the church environment. As we tried to listen to the sermon AJ had a complete meltdown and we panicked. Next to the window of the cry room was a note that read, "Please keep your children quiet-the glass is not soundproof."

We never went back to that church.

AJ attended a preschool that was about an hour from our home. The morning program was just over two hours so I saved my gas and drove around the city or hunkered down at the library. Every day for two years I passed this huge church on the county highway. *Holy buckets that thing is huge.* I felt a gentle calling to go back each time I passed the church. Attending a large church was never on my radar, but why not?

I will never forget my first visit to this church. It was huge and had a coffee bar. People were drinking coffee in the church. And there were bibles in the pews. No hymns. What is happening. While the service was great and we enjoyed ourselves, we were so shell-shocked it took us a while to return.

We began attending church there when AJ was in kindergarten. I took a huge leap and decided to attend a women's bible study group. Over the course of one summer we voyaged through Jennie Allen's *Stuck* study. I abruptly realized how incredibly stuck I was in my own life. The weekly work on my heart was hard but so desperately needed. The more I prayed and the more I cautiously opened up to these amazing women in my group, I was still stuck. Each week I asked for prayers for my heart to LET GO. Ask any of those women, even now, and they will tell you how angry I was then. Apparently I don't have a very good poker face.

It was a bright and sunny morning four years ago. I found myself is a sea of tears standing during the worship portion of our church service. No one noticed me, bawling upright, crying out to God to take the last flakes of bitterness at the bottom of my heart and blow them away. It was a crystal clear moment. I let it go. And I haven't looked back.

I can recall many, many, many conversations with myself over this very issue. My heart wasn't healed. I so desperately wanted it to be, but it just wasn't time. I have no idea why it took five years-but it did. No matter how many people told me to "get over it" or "it's not that bad" or "well, my child does this," I was still aching in pain. What I didn't realize that I was healing; God was healing me, a little at a time, as the years passed.

We began to feel ourselves surrounded by many of our friends who were adopting. Their love and passion for adoption is reminding me of those amazing moments WE experienced when we adopted AJ. How I didn't blink when traveling to a foreign country three times. How I didn't care about everyone else's opinions on how we were crazy. How extraordinary it was to love and miss this little boy I hadn't even met yet. How exciting it was to decorate his nursery. How overwhelming it felt when they placed him in our arms-forever. How full my heart was after a long trip home and watching him sleep in his crib for the very first time. All of these moments that were buried under such intense grief were front and center once again.

I know that faith is a touchy subject in the world of special needs. Some people want to punch God in the face, some are absolutely convinced he doesn't exist, and others rely on their faith wholeheartedly. I went from wanting to punch God in the face to realizing that I can't carry all of this on my own. I cannot express how freeing it is to be able to share the story of AJ coming home without barking "but we didn't know!" and ending my words with piercing bitterness. The bitterness has faded and has been replaced with thankfulness and opportunity. I'm thankful for the opportunity to bathe in God's incredible redemption and grace and know He loves me on the worst of days. When I curse the special needs my son's body fights every day He covers me in grace. When all my heart craves is to just be AJ's Mom, He reminds me that I AM.

CHAPTER 28

Dear Traveler

Dear Traveler,

I see you.

I see your face when you begin to wonder if something is going on with your child.

I see you in the shower crying silently as the water rushes over your tired body.

I see you as you hold a brave face for the doctor who is using big words you do not comprehend.

I see you hiding in your closet with chocolate and potato chips wishing this were easier.

I see you before your first IEP.

I see you on the phone with the insurance company, doctor's offices, and therapy clinics. I hear you discussing what your child needs and explaining way more than you should have to.

I see you guarding your child post-operation.

I see the crazy things you Google.

I see the way you and your husband deal with all of this differently.

I see you falling into bed only to wake in two hours.

I see you moving to different cities and states to find better treatments, school programming, and environments for your child.

I see you wondering why friends no longer call or stop by.

I see you grateful for friends who do and stop by and for the new friends too.

I see you thankful for that first step, word, or therapy goal met.

I see you educating yourself and those around you.

I see your tears of joy and your tears of sadness.

I see you pounding the pavement to get it done.

I see you dosing medications and doing exercises day in and day out.

I see you learning all that medical terminology and using it for good.

I see you doing things some cannot even imagine.

I see you fighting for everything your child needs.

I see you rejoicing in the little things and celebrating the victories.

I see you.

I will not tell you to buck up and deal with it. I will tell you it will be hard. And that my hard is probably not the same or going to be the same as your hard. That's okay. I will tell you your child will change your perspective and change your life. I will tell you how amazing this journey will be. It will stretch you, ground you, and grow you. Our children don't fit in a box and neither do we. We are still brothers and sisters. We share common ground. You will grow and learn, just as I did. You will find your people. You will educate yourself and advocate for your child…on your terms…in your way. You will find determination and strength you will find from a currently unknown source, because you just aren't there yet. But when the time comes, you will find that strength and pull up those boot straps and trudge along in the world with your child.

You will.

CHAPTER 29

Exit

The island of Molokai in Hawaii is a whopping thirty-five miles long. Jeremy and I spent an incredible two weeks on this small island a few years ago for our anniversary. Upon arrival at the tiny little airport we stepped into the car rental office to learn there were no convertibles left out of the handful of cars that were sitting on the red clay road.

"What do you mean?! I reserved a convertible!" I said.

"Well ma'am, I'm sorry. But we do have some Jeeps available.

Why would I want a Jeep? This is Hawaii for cripes sakes.

"Many of the roads and areas here require a Jeep with 4WD. I think you'll enjoy it."

"Fine."

Ugh. This is not what I planned.

"Is there a GPS in the Jeep?" I asked.

The woman behind the counter laughed.

"Molokai is only 38 miles long. There is one road. You'll be fine."

"Oh. Okay."

My mom likes to tell the story of when I was bit by a dog when I was six. Specifically, how while I was in the emergency room I was rapid-firing questions at the doctors and nurses while they were preparing my forehead with numbing medication before stitches. My mom called out, "You better tell her what you're doing or she won't calm down."

"What's her name?" the doctor said.

"Heidi."

"Okay, Heidi. Right now we are…."

I like to know things. Specifically, I like to know **all** the things and be able to project all the possibilities. Clearly this is part of my DNA. For me to be on a foreign island with no plan and no GPS sounded like a nightmare. I was straight up panicked. It may seem incredibly silly and humorous. Clearly the woman behind the counter found humor in my Type A planner brain. Even though I was clueless, she seemed to know just what I needed.

We spent the next few weeks without a schedule, plan, or agenda. I'm not so sure I've ever felt so free. Indeed there was only one completely paved road from one end of the island to the other. One morning we ventured to the Waikolu Overlook. As we turned off the main road the landscape changed several times over. The pavement turned to asphalt which then turned to gravel. The gravel was followed by thick and beautiful red clay. As we found ourselves higher in elevation the terrain reminded me more of a scene from Twilight than Hawaii. All of it was breathtaking. The drive pushed us out of our comfort zones and forced us to breathe in the beauty around us. The cover for this book was shot on the road coming back down from the lookout. I saw the view behind me in the rear-view mirror and asked Jeremy to stop so I could take the picture. Robert Frost's quote came to my mind the moment I stepped out of the car. Two roads.

I don't have to know everything. Detours are beautiful and can change us, for the better. AJ has certainly changed me and I like to think it has been for the better. How we "got" him doesn't matter anymore. His disabilities don't matter anymore. He's here and is my beautiful little boy. He keeps me centered and focused on what is truly important. He has given me tremendous perspective. He was unexpected, but steered my heart on a road with more love than I ever could have imagined. There is no real exit to our story. But detours? Detours are beautiful and can change all of us, for the better.

PS

Our social worker Deb called on a Friday afternoon.

Why is she calling me...with another question of some sort?

I had just spoken to her two weeks before to get the ball rolling with another international adoption.

"So, we received an email from another agency. They are looking for a family for this little girl."

"Ok."

I still wasn't getting the picture.

"They have a short deadline. They need to find her a family in the next week or her case goes back into the system. They are asking cooperating agencies if any of their families are interested.

"What?!"

"Here is some general information about her...."

"Uh huh. Uh huh." (Writing furiously on our white board.)

"I have to warn you, this agency is very conservative as to what type of families they will accept.

"Translation—they may not accept us due to Jer's medical stuff."

"It is a possibility. Let me see if I can get more information for you. In the meantime, I will let them know you are potentially interested. Sound good?"

"Ooooookey dok."

Click.

"Jer!!!!!!"

I stared at all of the scribbles on our white board and our patio table. Glass tiles work well as a writing surface when you are desperate.

The next day our conversation continued.

"I was able to obtain more information on this little girl."

I squash more writing in between the previous day's scribbles. I ask more questions as she spits out more and more information.

"Are you still interested?"

"Yes!"

"Let's have you send the medical letters you obtained for Jeremy to me and I will forward them to the agency."

"I can do that."

"The director has already asked to see your old home study."

"Holy buckets."

"I will let you know what they say."

"Ok!"

An email appears in my inbox.

"Here is the referral information. Please let me know ASAP if you are interested and would like to proceed."

"Are you joking? Are they ok with us?"

"They are open to you!"

GASSPPPPPPPPPP!

Do I open the attachments? Do I not?

I decided to open her general medical information first.

Jeremy called just as I was opening her photos and videos. I was instantly reminded of the moment we received AJ's referral.

Tears streamed down my cheeks as I saw her precious face. She is beautiful. I opened one picture first and then watched her live in a video.

I read the rest of her reports. I watched all of the videos and the picture slideshow over and over and over.

Is this really happening?

AJ had fallen asleep on the guest bed, so I had some time let this marinate.

I called our social worker and told her we wanted to pursue this sweet girl.

"Call the agency directly and speak to Molli. She will tell you the next steps."

(Shaking) "Ok."

"Hello Heidi! This is Molli. I'm so glad to finally talk to you! You and Jeremy have such expertise and such experience.

What?!

"Why thank you."

"What I want you to do is think this all over. You know the ropes. Take her information and share with doctors, specialists, etc. Then let me know your decision."

"I will do so."

"So glad we touched base!"

"Me too. This is CRAZY."

Click.

Just a few days later Molli called. They needed a decision.

We made the decision to accept her referral.

She was meant to be our daughter.

God is good. He is faithful.

He is carrying us down this new road.

Acknowledgements

Oh the many detours this book has been on. What started as a little project of mine while AJ was in preschool has spanned the course of six years. I sat down in a big comfy chair at the library and began writing the first chapter. I thought writing a book was an insane idea. This book has sat on the highway of my life in bumper to bumper traffic. It has been sidelined more times than I can count and ignored with feelings of ineptness and fear. I'm beyond grateful my life has finally brought this book to tangibility.

Jeremy: I love you. Who would have ever imagined this life we have today. I love that you're my opposite. Thank heavens we are never on the same wavelength, or we'd both be total messes. Thank you for believing I had a story to share with others. Thank you for your constant encouragement and flexibility with my creative heart.

AJ and Mimi: This story is one I never could have imagined. I love both of you with all of my heart and hope you find truth and understanding in these words. Sometimes life isn't fair. It is good, bad, ugly, and beautiful. May you grow into your own stories and live beautifully no matter what road you take. I love you.

Mom: Thanks for being you. You taught me to chase after my dreams, even when they were ridiculous by the world's standards. When I failed, you encouraged me to keep trying or to change course. Recalculating was always ok in your book. You have always encouraged my heart. Thank you.

Judy: Thank you for your whisper of confidence just when I needed it most. You were in the back of my mind throughout this entire process.

Gram: Here it is. I wish I could send a copy to you in Heaven. I never married the doctor or the lawyer, nor did I become a journalist or lawyer as you suggested. I still argue like a boss though, so don't you worry. I did marry a Nurse Practitioner and began a career as a writer, so let's call that a compromise.

To Erik: Thank you for your unwavering support and encouragement when this delicate student was so torn down. You planted a seed for English and writing that has never ceased.

To Michele: You are the sweetest person I have ever known. Sweet, with more grit and integrity than I ever thought was possible in a human. You covered me in grace and understanding when I needed it the most.

To Leslie: THE greatest physical therapist on the planet. Nothing I say here will even begin to express my thanks for all you have done for AJ and for our family. What began as a rocky relationship between you and I blossomed into a continuous friendship. You were AJ's greatest advocate and never let me fall on my fears for his future. You built my confidence and strengthened my advocacy for AJ to infinity and beyond.

To Les, Mary Ellen, Annette, Kathy, Ashley, Mick, Rona, Linda, Chris, Nancy, Amy B., Dione, Sarah, Hilary, Deb S., Kelli, Maria,

Karen, Kathryn, Megan, Denise, Lisa, Bill, Bev, Nicki, Deb K., Karen P., Julie, Debbie J., Kelly, Lindsey, Kate, Dedra, Becky, Becca, Abby, Jenna, Kristin, Maggie, Lia, Priscilla, Anna, and Kathy R.: All of you are so very precious. Each of you knows that when you enter AJ's life or our family's life you become family. I am so grateful. Someday there will be additional words to express gratitude beyond the standard *thank you*. Until then, know you are a magnitude of blessings sprinkled on our family.

To WestBow Press and my sweet coordinator Barb: Thank you for hosting the writing contest that sent this project into full throttle. Barb-you deserve a medal for the overabundance of patience you had with me during this process. Thank you.

To Liz Gilbert: Who encouraged me and the rest of the world to *just write*. Who speaks to my heart and says you can do this and you don't have to have all your stuff together. Thank you.

To Brenda Warner: Thank you for sharing your story and making me feel less alone. I've never forgotten that conference or your words.

To Jen Hatmaker: Who knew how being part of your launch team would change my life and breathe life back into this book. Thank you for the opportunity, your sweet hospitality, and your candor.

To the FTL Launch Team: Tribe! Thank you for being a safe place and for sharing His love in such incredible ways. Y'all have inspired me.

To Carrie: Thank you for that coffee conversation that sparked and continues to ignite my passion for transparency. It is my deepest wish that this book will replicate the conversation we had that day, many times over, for many others.

To Mol: You got a whole chapter so you get a short sentence. I love you.

To Kyle: You read the first draft and sent me the most encouraging note afterward. I have that sucker printed and reference it often. Your response helped me realize writing this book truly held the opportunity to influence others. Your words encouraged me that all of this hard work would be worth it.

To Becky and Debbie: You ladies are my heroes. You are real life writers in my circle of friends that make this writer thing feel tangible and achievable. Thank you for your mentorship.

To Kelly, Becky, and Amy: I'm thankful for your eyeballs, critiques, and red marks all over my many, many drafts.

To my launch team: From the bottom of my heart, thank you for being a part of this project. Thank you for your encouragement, opinions, time, and precious efforts. Thank you for sharing this book with the world.

Printed in the United States
By Bookmasters